To Dawn ?
Steve

Thank you!
ministry to so m
Thanks for being...
Valient for Truth!

Christy Stilymn
Job 12:20

Christy Chavers Stutzman

THE SPIRITUAL PRICE OF POLITICAL SILENCE

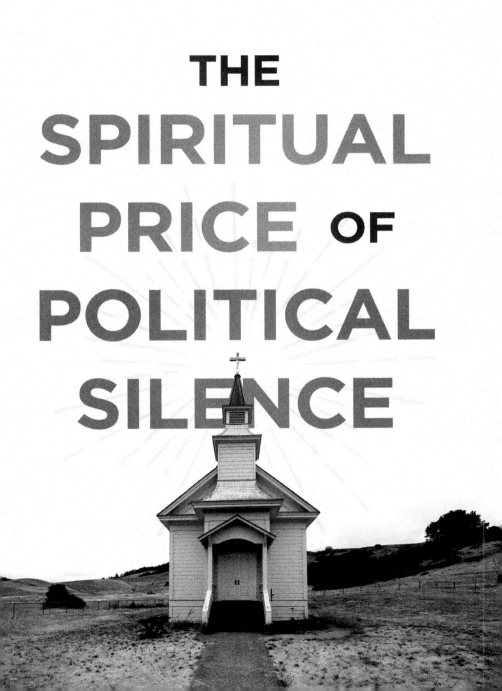

"This book is not just timely, it is essential reading for every person of faith in America today. Christy Stutzman's summary of our Judeo/Christian history, her clear explanation of our journey to moral decline, and her practical presentation of how and why people of faith must be involved in the public arena is brilliantly presented. If we want to reclaim America's spiritual birthright, we now have a roadmap to do so"
—Rachel Campos Duffy-Author & Host of Fox and Friends Weekend Fox News Channel

"Every one of our Founding Fathers knew that for America to be successful, it would require a "virtuous" people. Christy Stutzman's book — 'The Spiritual Price of Political Silence' makes the case that a 'virtuous' people is even more necessary in today's world."
—US Senator Rand Paul

"Complacency has consequences. The Spiritual Price of Political Silence eloquently captures the universal sentiments echoing across nations-America has long been a beacon of light, its foundation rooted in Judeo-Christian beliefs that have illuminated our path. However, ominous tremors now shake our once-solid footing, as political and cultural conflicts erode the voices and values that once radiated America's brilliance. Christy's remarkable book serves as a clarion call, urging us to realize the cost of remaining silent amidst political turmoil. Time is of the essence, for both America and the world. Let us not succumb to darkness."
—Melissa Ohden - Abortion Survivors Network Founder, Author of *You Carried Me: A Daughter's Memoir*

"President John Adams once wrote, *'Facts are stubborn things.'* Facts establish truth, and this book is full of both historical and practical truth. In *The Spiritual Price of Political Silence*, you will not only be inspired and encouraged with hope for our nation but also presented with a practical plan for how to achieve positive change."
—David Barton- American Historian,
Founder & President of WallBuilders

"I am convinced that the concerns we have about the decline of our country can be influenced by the involvement of local churches and individual Christians. Christy Stutzman analyzes the history of church participation in the political process from the founding of our country, explains the desperate need for Christian involvement to stop the moral decay in our culture and gives ways the reader can engage to make a difference. I highly recommend "The Spiritual Price of Political Silence" for all who care about the future of our country."
—Monica Kelsey. Founder & CEO
of Safe Haven Baby Boxes, Inc.

"A clarion call to action, this book reminds all American people of faith that we still have the power to correct our course. "The Spiritual Price is Political Silence" is an honest assessment of our past, present and future. You will be armed with facts, hope, and the knowledge you need to be an effective agent for renewing America's purpose: to be a light to the world. At this time of crisis, Christy Stutzman provides the refreshing reminder we all need that our birthright of freedom still belongs to the people."
—Dave Brat, Former US Congressman & Dean of the
School of Business at Liberty University

"I have known Christy Stutzman now for just over 12 years. She has never ceased to amaze me in her life of being a great wife to her husband, and a terrific mother to her two sons. Whether it's music, politics or understanding of the world in which we live... she has always been able to assess where we are...and what we should do if we want it to be changed. She has done it again with "The Spiritual Price of Political Silence" an essential resource for those who fear our nation is in decline. It's a glimmer of hope and a guidebook for American's of faith. Filled with refreshing reminders about our Judeo-Christian heritage, Christy uses this book to inspire us all, and prepare us to be ready to re-engage the culture, to "be valiant for truth," and to renew America's global purpose. That's a lot to ask of one book...but this one delivers."
—Pat Miller, Radio Host of The Pat Miller Program, WOWO Newstalk 1190 AM

End Game Press books may be purchased in bulk at special discounts for sales promotion, corporate gifts, ministry, fund-raising, or educational purposes. Special editions can also be created to specifications. For details, contact Special Sales Dept., End Game Press, P.O. Box 206, Nesbit, MS 38651 or info@endgamepress.com.

Visit our website at www.endgamepress.com.

Library of Congress Control Number: 2023933559
Hardback ISBN: 978-1-63797-151-2
Ebook ISBN: 978-1-63797-166-6

Printed in India
10 9 8 7 6 5 4 3 2 1

Dedicated to:
My husband, Marlin, who has been tested, proven,
and found faithful in the battle for liberty as a trusted
public servant, father, and man of God.

In memory of my father, Nicky Chavers, who loved
studying the hand of God in history and infused me
with that same passion.

And to my two sons, Payton & Preston-
May you always be men of principled action and forever
- Valiant for Truth!

PREFACE

This book is written to my fellow Americans who hold deep faith in the Holy Scriptures and the Judeo-Christian principles on which our nation was founded. It is written to those who see the state of our nation and feel overwhelmed, discouraged, and brokenhearted. It is written to those who have their entire future ahead of them, but who view it with doubt and concern instead of the historic American optimism that has always been a part of our national attitude.

This book is for those who identify with the words of the psalmist who wrote in Psalm 77 (KJV):

> *I have considered the days of old, the years of ancient times ... Will the Lord cast off forever? and will he be favourable no more? ... And I said, This is my infirmity: but I will remember the years of the right hand of the most High. I will remember the works of the LORD: surely I will remember Thy wonders of old. ... Thou art the God that doest wonders: Thou hast declared Thy strength among the people.*[1]

This book is written to those who know the true history of America and her founding documents. It is written to those who seek to follow God earnestly and sincerely, who may have been discouraged from taking part in the political process, and who may be disillusioned with the declining moral state of our beloved nation.

Although we recognize that the lives of the Founding Fathers who labored and sacrificed their "lives, fortunes and sacred honor" in order to craft our unique form of government were not perfect, as people of faith, we understand that no one is perfect, and that God intervenes in the lives of imperfect people to accomplish His will in spite of our failings.

It is good to remind ourselves that the list of imperfect people in Scripture is long, and yet, over the centuries, God has used broken, sinful people in miraculous ways to accomplish His purposes. As I look back on those who sacrificed greatly to give us our birthright of liberty, I write this book in hopes that we will offer ourselves as willing, yet imperfect vessels to be used of Him in our generation, to be a light in this dark world as so many have done before us.

We must not doubt the truth of what is behind us, and we must also recognize what is now transpiring before our eyes. We must be willing to acknowledge both the good and the bad of the past as well as that of the present. We must not fail to acknowledge that the ultimate goal of those who wrote and created the founding documents and crafted our unique form of government was to create a nation based on God's divine moral law. They clearly stated in their writings and numerous debates that in order for the free exercise of God-given liberties to be enjoyed, the laws passed by the government would have to be based on the moral law of God, creating orderly bounds for the exercise of that liberty.

Our Constitution and Bill of Rights clearly recognize the right of every man to rule himself, but our founders also emphasized the responsibility of every man to fulfill his duties to society according to the "laws of nature and of nature's God."[2] The growing awareness that existed at the time of America's founding regarding individual responsibility and accountability to God was a key principle that guided the creation of a new form of government, one that would be reliant on that key concept of every individual having a personal relationship with God. The forming of the American government paired the laws of nature's God with the God-given rights of every individual as a powerful combination of foundational truths, guiding the decisions of the founders regarding the construction of the government. We should celebrate the fact that their goal, to create a system of accountability, a balance of limited governmental powers, the blessing and responsibility of self-governance, and the free exercise of individual conscience was realized!

As we stand looking back now on two and a half centuries of existence, it is clear that their grand experiment in self-government has triumphed more than the founders could have ever imagined. Yes, it was ugly at times. It was tragic and difficult and left us with national scars that still need healing; yet there is no doubt that the victories have far outweighed the losses and that the triumphs have far outweighed the tragedies.

I write this book to those who understand the fact that our forefathers worked tirelessly to create a government in which power was given to the people to correct our own mistakes and to "form a more perfect union."[3] They gave us the means to govern ourselves and find solutions to our own societal failings if we would have the will and understanding to do so. We, the people, were empowered to self-govern and were even given the chance to serve as citizen leaders, but only by the consent of the governed for a limited period of time. In describing our form of government, the American's Creed says it best:

> A government of the people, by the people, for the people; whose just powers are derived by the consent of the governed, a democracy within a republic a sovereign Nation of many sovereign States; a perfect union, one and inseparable; established upon those principles of freedom, equality, justice, and humanity for which American patriots sacrificed their lives and fortunes.[4]

Through the careful diligence and wisdom of those whom I call the Authors of American Liberty, every American, regardless of ancestry, social status, race, or ethnicity, was given a government which would allow for debate, the confrontation of societal wrongs, and a means to correct those wrongs. With time, it allowed every American the means to participate in this incredible system of self-government—if they chose to do so.

This book is written to my fellow Americans who stand firm on Biblical principles. It is my prayer that this remnant might be armed with truth and courage to save and preserve liberty for the next generation and that they might fan the flame of liberty into a light that shines with hope and truth throughout the world.

CHAPTER ONE

THE ENTIRE WORLD IS WATCHING

The view from the top of the hill was breathtaking. It was a site I had only dreamed of seeing and I was still pinching myself, trying to believe this was happening. Standing in a small group, we gazed at the view of the idyllic Sea of Galilee from the Mount of Beatitudes. Most of the members of our group were just trying to take it all in. This is where Jesus had spoken the words we had all memorized in Sunday School as children, words we had tried to emulate with our lives. We stood in awe and could almost hear His words echo across the hillside as we gazed in wonder: *"Blessed are the poor in spirit: for theirs is the kingdom of Heaven. Blessed are they that mourn: for they shall be comforted. Blessed are the meek: for they shall inherit the earth"* (Matthew 5:3-5, KJV).

It was a sweet moment of reflection and realization, standing close to where Christ had stood as He taught the multitudes so long ago. We glanced at each other knowingly, since many of us had met together for prayer or Bible studies in the previous months. Our Israeli guide had made it very clear to us that he was Jewish by birth and an Israeli citizen, but he was "not religious." Yet the insights he shared were presented with great understanding of both the Jewish and Christian faiths. As we stood there gazing at the beautiful site, he started to speak, and what he said next laid the foundation for the twelve-year journey which led me to write this book.

He took out a Bible and asked if one of us would be willing to read the Sermon on the Mount in Matthew 5—the very words which Jesus had spoken at that spot. My husband eagerly volunteered. Our group formed a circle under the shade of the chapel which overlooks the beautiful Sea of Galilee and listened to my husband read that familiar passage, and it was as if we were hearing it for the first time. After he finished, there was a moment's pause, and then the guide spoke again. "Could you please go back and read verses thirteen through sixteen?" he asked. My husband then read:

> Ye are the salt of the earth: but if the salt have lost his savor, wherewith shall it be salted? It is thenceforth good for nothing, but to be cast out, and to be trodden under foot of men. Ye are the light of the world. A city that is set on an hill cannot be hid. Neither do men light a candle, and put it under a bushel, but on a candlestick; and it giveth light unto all that are in the house.
>
> Let your light so shine before men, that they may see your good works and glorify your Father which is in heaven. (Matthew 5:13-16, KJV)

Our guide looked intently at our group and said, "I know that you are all members of the United States Congress and that you make important decisions every day. I want you to know that I believe America has followed this teaching of Jesus. America has done this thing that Jesus said. You have been this 'light to the world.' But I want to beg you, as American leaders: please … don't stop. My country and the entire world needs you to continue to be this light for the world. If you stop, I don't see any other country on the face of the globe that will do the same. Please, don't stop."

There was silence. The smiles and wonder we all had been sharing turned to gentle tears and heavy hearts, as we realized the truth of what he had just said. I will never forget the feeling of monumental responsibility that fell on our shoulders at that moment. Our guide was right in his assessment, and he was right in his request. America *had* been a light to the world from her very beginning!

There we stood, members of the United States Congress and their spouses; but more than that, as the church and as people of faith, hearing a plea from someone who had seen the light of hope, truth, and liberty coming from our nation, who was asking us to continue the work.

The Fulfillment of a Dream

After hearing that plea from our Israeli guide, so many thoughts came rushing into my mind: lessons from American history, warnings from leaders in the church, and prayers that had been prayed for America. Our guide had done two things at once. He had confirmed the fulfillment of the hopes and prayers of countless Americans for centuries, and he had confirmed the fact that America's decline was on full display.

It reminded me of a quote from *Of Plymouth Plantation.* In his history, Governor William Bradford wrote of the perilous journey that the little band of Separatists (Pilgrims) had undertaken. He clearly articulated the reason that drove them to leave everything they had ever known to start a new life in the New World. They were willing to endure unimaginable dangers and the countless hardships of carving out a new life in a rugged new world because they had "a great hope and inward zeal of laying some good foundation, or at least to make some way thereunto, for propagating and advancing the Gospel of the kingdom of Christ in those remote parts of the world.[5] That little band of people, as our guide had stated, had "done this thing that Jesus said."

The Mayflower Compact came to mind. Due to treacherous weather conditions and other mitigating factors, the Pilgrims were forced to settle in an area of the continent which had not been agreed upon by their financiers. They had no official charter or authority from the King for the area where they had landed, and so in the absence of any formal legal authority, they wrote the Mayflower Compact in an effort to establish order and to serve as an initial form of government. Although they were a combined group of those known as Separatists along with a few families and individuals who had simply come to seek a new life with new opportunities, what they wrote in the Mayflower Compact speaks clearly to their united purpose for coming to the new world:

> **IN THE NAME OF GOD, AMEN**. We, whose names are underwritten, the Loyal Subjects of our dread Sovereign Lord King *James*, by the Grace of God, of *Great Britain*, *France*, and *Ireland*, King, *Defender of the Faith*, &c. Having undertaken for the Glory of God, and Advancement of the Christian Faith, and the Honour of our King and Country, a Voyage to plant the first Colony in the northern Parts of *Virginia*; Do by these Presents, solemnly and mutually, in the Presence of God and one another, covenant and combine ourselves together into a civil Body Politick, for our better Ordering and Preservation, and Furtherance of the Ends aforesaid (emphasis added).[6]

The Pilgrims and other groups who came to America seeking religious freedom understood that they were merely stepping stones. That first generation of original colonists, fleeing religious persecution from all over the known world, were united in hope that the foundation that they laid would someday result in the true light of God shining from the shores of America throughout the entire world.

Governor Bradford lived long enough to be able to write, "Just as one small candle may light a thousand, so the light here kindled hath shone unto many."[7]

My mind then turned to the words of Governor John Winthrop, the Puritan governor of the Massachusetts colony, who challenged the people of his colony to follow God wholeheartedly and reminded them that they would be "like a city upon a hill," in reference, again, to Matthew 5. He told his congregations that they needed to be aware that "The eyes of all people are upon us" and they should strive to live peaceably and righteously with God and with each other.[8]

As the great migration continued through the mid 1600s, those seeking asylum from religious persecution were instrumental in writing the founding documents of the colonies. In 1643, the colonists of New England wrote these words into their constitution, repeating the same reasons cited by the Pilgrims in coming to America:

> Whereas we all came to these parts of America with the same end and aim, namely, to advance the kingdom of our Lord Jesus Christ, and to enjoy the liberties of the Gospel thereof with purities and peace, and for preserving and propagating the truth and liberties of the gospel.[9]

Their efforts were sincere but sometimes flawed, as they sought to exercise their natural liberties while carving out an existence in an untamed land. As the different colonies grew and expanded, they were tested in their attempts to govern themselves while balancing the freedom of conscience and expression they had risked so much to enjoy.

The Worldwide Reach of America's Faith

It took several generations for the colonies to stabilize and begin to prosper in freedom. It was almost two hundred years later, in 1812, when Adoniram Judson, America's first foreign missionary, set sail for the distant shores of Burma (now Myanmar). With his journey from the shores of America to the distant shores of Burma for the express purpose of sharing the gospel, the second part of the vision "of propagating the truth and liberties of the gospel" that the Pilgrims and other people of faith had brought to the shores of America finally became a reality. That vision would continue to be a reality for the next two hundred years.

Still lost in thought after hearing the heartfelt plea from my Israeli guide, I recalled the names of Christian missionaries down through the centuries: David Brainerd, Lottie Moon, Jim and Elisabeth Elliott, Nate Saint, and so many others. Those Americans had sacrificed greatly to carry the light of the gospel and the love of God from the shores of America to the ends of the earth. They had "done this thing that Jesus said."

Clara Barton's incredible work with the Red Cross for millions in crisis around the world had "done this thing that Jesus said."

US presidents who spoke boldly of their faith and members of Congress who stood for righteous causes over the years had "done this thing that Jesus said."

GIs who risked their very lives to liberate Europe from oppression and dictatorships and who had shown compassion for those they liberated had "done this thing that Jesus said."

Billy Graham and his worldwide evangelistic efforts had been a light to the world. In recent years, hundreds of thousands of American Christians, including my own family, have participated in Operation Christmas Child with Samaritan's Purse, founded by Franklin Graham, and together, as American Christians, we were a small part of being that light.

American-funded missions, charities, disaster relief organizations, rescue operations, schools, church planting efforts, Bible translators, radio broadcasts, missions, seminaries, and so much more had been a part of being a light to the world. They had "done this thing that Jesus said."

As I stood where Christ had given the Sermon on the Mount, I reflected on the spiritual legacy and ongoing responsibility that we have as Americans. It was almost surreal to hear a citizen of another country, however unknowingly, confirm that the vision of the Pilgrims of 1620, the Puritans of 1630, the Quakers of Pennsylvania and Delaware, the Baptist founders of Rhode Island, the Catholics of Maryland, the Methodists and Presbyterians of the Southern states, and the immigrants from all over the world who had fled to America for a chance to live according to their conscience and convictions, had been realized. It was an overwhelming joy!

In that moment, I knew that our nation was not just seen in light of our current president, our material wealth, our advancements in technology, or our military strength. Citizens of other nations had observed something more than all that about us. They had observed something about the United States of America that emanated from the hearts of the American people themselves.

Realizing What the World Sees Now

These encouraging thoughts were a comfort, but soon turned to a sad realization which begged the question: Why was this man concerned that our light might not continue? When tasked with guiding a US Congressional delegation on a tour of Biblical sites in Israel, why did he feel so concerned about the decline of our country that he was compelled to go off script to make a personal plea to people whom he believed could do something about it?

The answer was clear. The American light was growing dim and the world was watching it fade. I believe that the world is still watching that light as it flickers and fades because they understand something that we might have forgotten: *The spiritual and moral health of America does not only affect our country. It affects the world.*

There are experiences in life that are worth repeating in an effort to encourage others. I experienced quite a poignant moment the first time that my husband and I were allowed to enter the chamber of the US House of Representatives. I will never forget it.

We had come through our election and had arrived in Washington not knowing what to expect when we arrived. Each freshman class of Congress is given about a week's worth of orientation, and ours began with a beautiful dinner served in the amazingly elegant Statuary Hall in the US Capitol. It is the original room where the House of Representatives used to meet, and it is filled with statues of great Americans down through the centuries.

We were seated at large round tables with other freshman members of Congress from around the country. We each went around and introduced ourselves. I remember meeting Colonel Allen West from Florida and his wife, Angela; Scott Tipton, a pottery maker from Colorado, and his wife, Jean; former NFL player Jon Runyan from New Jersey and his wife, Loretta; and small businessman Bill Huizenga from Michigan and his wife, Natalie, who were all seated at our table that first night.

Being a part of the largest freshman class elected to Congress in over seventy years, we were overwhelmed as we looked around us at the beautiful setting. With the likenesses and statues of America's legends, heroes, and leaders such as John Winthrop, William Penn, Daniel Webster, John Quincy Adams, Davy Crockett, Lew Wallace, Patrick Henry, and many of the Founding Fathers, we sat down to dinner for the first time as members of Congress. As we stood to welcome the newly elected Speaker of the House, I glanced around at the images of the great Americans who had gone before us. They seemed to look right back at us through their marble exteriors, watching with apprehensive hope. It was as though they knew the battle before us and were straining to break through time's prison bars to help us.

At that moment, I felt as if time stood still, and I was experiencing a moment in history similar to those experienced by other nations at turning points in the annals of time: Egypt, Israel, Greece, Rome, Great Britain, and others. And yet, this moment was different than the rest of history's turning points because the American story is different. It is unique in the history of the world.

As I thought of our family's story, and then the stories of many who were there, I couldn't help but stand in awe of the miracle that is America. There were farmers, carpenters, car salesmen, and pottery makers. There were former professional athletes and there were Army colonels and officers. We came from all walks of life, many ethnicities, and different economic circumstances, but we had all come, most having never met before, and found ourselves agreed on one thing: We had been sent by the people to serve the people—nothing more, and certainly nothing less.

As I looked around at the smiling but intensely focused faces of those who had come with eager hearts to serve America that evening, I felt the weight of that task fall squarely on the shoulders of those of us in that room. It hit us all. Surrounded by a cloud of witnesses, commissioned to serve the people, we knew what we had come to do, and at that moment, our records would begin. They were watching from above, they were watching from without, and we prayed in that moment that God would see fit to watch us and guide us from within as well.

The First Act in Congress

It was fitting, then, when the Speaker asked all of us to follow him down the hall, to "get a first look" at the Chamber of the House of Representatives (for many of us, it would be the first time in our lives that we had viewed it), that there was a hush among us, and after a few minutes of gazing at the beautiful room and taking some pictures at the Speaker's rostrum, I noticed a small group of four sitting to the side, and then a group of six in the back, with heads bowed, some holding hands, quietly and fervently praying together.

Some stood before large paintings of Washington, gazing at his face as if trying to glean wisdom from his expression; yet so many prayed—quietly, humbly, sincerely—seeking the blessing and guidance of the Divine Providence who had led our Fathers in their quest for freedom and had brought us together to continue the great work of liberty. They prayed intensely, sitting in the seats that they would soon fill as Representatives of their friends and neighbors.

It was a quiet act that not many people will ever hear about or read about. No reporters were there to take pictures or document the moment, but I will carry that image with me for as long as I live. It is my prayer that something similar has happened with each successive group of freshmen.

A Prayer for Continued Strength and Vigilance

It is also my prayer that something similar will happen each time we turn on the news, go to a parent-teacher meeting, attend a community gathering, or stand in line at the polls to vote. I hope we pray and seek the God who has preserved our beloved nation so that He might continue to bless America.

The world is watching us. That cloud of witnesses who sacrificed so much to give us a free nation is watching us from the battlements of heaven. Our children are watching us. And most of all, God is watching us.

Whether we fully understand it or not, America's unique role in the world is the direct result of our Judeo-Christian roots and the incredible sacrifices of countless people of faith. They did so for a chance to accomplish two vital missions:

1. To live in obedience to God and raise their families according to their own consciences.
2. To shine God's light of truth throughout the entire world.

The fact is that the bedrock of our nation has been under attack for so long that it is starting to crumble, and the cracks are very visible. Today, we face a decision point as people of faith in America. We must answer the following questions honestly and with the proper understanding of our history:

1. What role did faith play in the founding of America?
2. When and why did American Christians begin to lose our influence?
3. Should Christians and people of faith be involved in American politics today?
4. What is our role now, in this present crisis of American decline?
5. Are we too late to make a difference?

In recent decades, these questions have been debated in American circles and the conclusions have been diverse and inconsistent. Were our founders really Christians? Was America founded on Judeo-Christian principles, or was it based on Deistic philosophies espoused by leading voices like Jefferson, Paine, and others who were heavily inspired by the philosophers of the Enlightenment? After reading original documents and studying the Founders in their own words, the answer is abundantly clear.

In the following chapters, I want to give you a brief summary of that evidence. It is thrilling to discover the rich mine of our spiritual heritage, filled with treasures that I hope will encourage your heart. Each subsequent chapter will answer the questions listed above and, by the end, it is my prayer that you will be armed with the truth of our founding, with resources to continue studying on your own, and the knowledge of how you can be best informed, engaged, and involved in keeping America's light shining to all the world.

CHAPTER TWO

THE ROLE OF FAITH IN AMERICA'S FOUNDING

There is no doubt that those who formed the various colonial governments of the original colonies in the early 1600s, and those who later formed America's national government in the late 1700s, were heavily inspired, influenced, and guided by their dedication and mutual reverence for the traditional Christian faith and the Holy Scriptures. In his book *America's Christian Heritage*, Gary DeMar writes that our "nation begins not in 1776, but more than one hundred fifty years earlier."[10]

In his article for the Heritage Foundation titled, "Did America Have a Christian Founding?", Professor Mark David Hall writes:

> By almost any measure, colonists of European descent who settled in the New World were serious Christians whose constitutions, laws, and practices reflected the influence of Christianity.[11]

The first wave of colonists to create permanent settlements on the shores of what would eventually become the United States of America had come after being convicted by their own study of the Scriptures. There were others who came seeking wealth, land, and adventure as well, but the largest groups of immigrants were those seeking religious freedom. Their dedication to their faith and the practice of their convictions had been met with great persecution by rulers across Europe who still held antiquated views of forcing citizens to belong to the state-approved church. Over the centuries, what had begun as a well-meaning effort on the part of Christian rulers to ensure adherence to the Christian faith had become a dictatorial nightmare for the common man.

Although most of Europe was deeply committed to the Christian faith, the only copies of the Bible were made by the church and were in Latin, a language known only to church scholars and the ruling elite. The work of Bible translators like Wycliffe, Tyndale, d'Étaples, Lefèvre, Luther and others who risked their own lives to translate the Bible into the common language had a profound effect on the European population.

When Gutenberg invented the printing press and scholars began printing the Bible in the common languages, the people could read and interpret the Bible for themselves. Soon there began a movement away from the established state churches and toward a deeper understanding of the dictates of conscience and the individual convictions of faith practices.

Many sects of Christianity emerged outside the established state churches, which meant a loss of state church control and power. Persecution of dissenters became rampant. No longer were priests and monks and cardinals the interpreters of the Scriptures for a people kept in ignorance and reliant on the church for understanding the teachings of the Bible. Religious freedom had a new meaning, and people were desperate to find a place where they would be allowed to live and worship God in peace and freedom.

In the early 1600s, various religiously devout groups began to arrive on American shores, committed to establishing a form of government which would allow for reasoned dissent, equitable representation, and above all, freedom of religion.

I share this because there has been a long, concerted effort to downplay the true motivations of the early settlers in America. Humanist historians have even tried to change the story and character of the Pilgrims of 1620. So let's look at just one of the many original documents these early freedom seekers left behind.

Of Pilgrims, Puritans & Patriots

The Mayflower Compact begins with the words "In the name of God, Amen," and refers to their motivations in establishing the settlement as being "for the Glory of God and advancement of the Christian faith."[12]

When we think of the Pilgrims, we think of the first Thanksgiving and the funny hats and outfits that they wore. But when you read their actual story, it reads like an action-adventure novel! Let's dig a little deeper into the incredible Pilgrim story. Their influence on our American culture was immeasurable, but the depth of their sacrifice is unimaginable.

Under threat of severe persecution and even death, the little congregation at Scrooby Manor in England began meeting together in their own homes to study the Bible for themselves. Through diligent study, they were convicted to worship God according to the dictates of their own consciences and soon faced persecution from their government.

One of their members was a teenage boy named William Bradford who eventually wrote the definitive history of the Pilgrims in his book, *Of Plymouth Plantation*. He recorded that in 1606, while facing great dangers, the little congregation at Scrooby made the following covenant together:

> the Lord's free people joined themselves (by a covenant of the Lord) into a church estate, in the fellowship of the gospel, to walk in all His ways made known or to be made known unto them, according to their best endeavors, whatsoever it should cost them, the Lord assisting them.[13]

If you read that final phrase of the covenant, "whatsoever it should cost them, the Lord assisting them," and then you read what actually happened to them as they attempted to follow the calling of God, you will realize that the price they paid was beyond what any of us could ever imagine being willing to pay. Imprisonments, property seizures, threats from authorities, the sale of lands and houses, secret escapes, treacherous ocean voyages, living in poverty in a different country, and finally risking everything to take a perilous, month-long journey across the Atlantic in a tiny vessel in the middle of winter—these were just the first parts of their story.

Once they arrived on American shores, they had no shelter, no means of warmth or provisions, and no understanding of the language of the people who inhabited the area where they had landed. From their search for land on which to build, to the miraculous assistance of Squanto and Massasoit, the hand of God provided miracle after miracle as they struggled to survive. They experienced starvation, plague, and the deaths of half of their group in the first year alone. By seeking peace with the Native Americans and learning new ways to survive, somehow they built the settlement at Plymouth and lived in peace with the Native Americans for many years. Bradford records that they saw themselves as stepping stones to establish a new land where men were free to worship God. They were clear in their vision of this new land being used as a beacon of hope and a light to all the world. This vision was not exclusive to the Pilgrims; as we will see, it was shared by thousands of new settlers to follow.

Ten years after the Pilgrims landed, John Winthrop led the journey of 700 Puritans in eleven ships in 1630. Some joined the settlement at Plymouth and others migrated north to settle the Massachusetts Bay colony and the city of Boston. In 1682, William Penn and his large groups of Quakers began settlements throughout Pennsylvania and Delaware. Amish and Mennonites came from Switzerland, Germany, and the Alsace-Lorraine area of Europe, settling in Pennsylvania and eventually moving west and south across the continent. Baptists and Methodists could be found in Virginia, the Carolinas, and Georgia around the same time the Quakers were arriving, and Maryland was a safe haven for Catholics seeking religious freedom as well. Those of the Jewish faith came to New York, New Jersey, and other northeastern settlements and were scattered throughout all thirteen colonies in the late 1600s and early 1700s. The diversity of those who immigrated to the shores of America seeking religious freedom is part of what made America great. They did not come in conquest for a king. These persecuted souls had been rejected and harassed by dictatorial governments and monarchs. They left all they had known to seek the freedom to live their lives in peace and safety. The role that faith played in forming the culture of the various settlements was a huge part of what led their descendents to seek independence in 1776. Yet, one hundred years before the Declaration of Independence was written, the great American experiment had already begun.

As we move forward a few years, we see the influence of faith in all thirteen colonies. The *Fundamental Orders of Connecticut*, often referred to as the first written constitution in the Western world, was heavily influenced by a sermon that well-respected minister, Reverend Thomas Hooker, gave on May 31, 1638. It was used as the framework for government in Connecticut from 1639 to 1662. It was also used as a model in the writing of the US Constitution and several other colonial constitutions. It began with this clear and bold statement of faith as its foundation:

> Forasmuch as it hath pleased the Almighty God by the wise disposition of his divine prudence that we the inhabitants ... are now cohabiting and dwelling in and upon the River of Connecticut ... and well knowing where a people are gathered together, the word of God requires that to maintain the peace and union of such a people, there should be an orderly and decent Government established according to God ... do for ourselves

and our Successors enter into Combination and Confederation together, to maintain and preserve the liberty
and purity of the Gospel of our Lord Jesus, which according to the truth of the said Gospel is now practiced
amongst us ... to be guided and governed according to
such Laws, Rules, Orders and decrees as shall be made,
ordered & decreed.[14]

Many other colonial charters, documents, and declarations use
similar language and reference specific Scripture passages.

The great reformers of Scotland and Switzerland taught a more
personal view of faith and the natural rights of man. Those who had
accepted these views and decided to find a new life across the ocean
came to the shores of America with a deep conviction regarding
the rights granted to them by their Creator and not any particular
church, king, ruler, or earthly government. This understanding of
natural rights given by God was a foundational principle in British
common law, but its application had become twisted by the establishment of a state church connected to the monarchy. Those British
citizens who came to America believed that religious freedom was a
natural right as well. This was highly agreed upon by the vast majority of early American colonists and was a key part of emboldening
their resolve to break with Britain and declare their independence
as a sovereign nation.

The first Great Awakening, led by the evangelistic preaching of
men like George Whitefield, brought many Americans to repentance from the outward practice of piety to an inward zeal to walk
with God. It was a national movement of true humility before God
and a return to prayer and fasting. Many of the Founding Fathers
who served in the Continental Congress in Philadelphia in 1776
had sat under the preaching of the great men who led the revivals
throughout the colonies.

Patriot leader, member of the Virginia House of Delegates,
and the first and sixth Governor of Virginia Patrick Henry said on

March 3, 1775, in his famous speech calling for action against the British invasion of the harbors:

> Sir, we are not weak if we make a proper use of those means which the God of nature hath placed in our power. Three millions of people, armed in the holy cause of liberty, and in such a country as that which we possess, are invincible by any force which our enemy can send against us. Besides, sir, we shall not fight our battles alone. There is a just God who presides over the destinies of nations; and who will raise up friends to fight our battles for us.[15]

Undeniable Evidence

One of the misleading teachings that Americans have believed is that the men who signed the Declaration of Independence, and those who fought in the American War for Independence, were breaking the Biblical teaching of living in obedience to rulers and earthly authorities. According to historical evidence and recorded documentation of the events as they happened, this is simply not true. The British colonists had lived under British common law, with all of its rights and freedoms, for over one hundred years, and when they petitioned their rulers regarding the infringements of their legal rights to representation and consent of the governed, they were not only ignored, but they were declared outside the protection of the monarch. They were considered enemies to their own government. To put it bluntly, their government had abandoned them and waged war against them before they ever declared independence. Boston had already been barricaded and the harbor blockaded, so by the time the Declaration was signed, George Washington was in New York, commanding a ragtag army of men simply trying to defend themselves against British aggression. This is why he was not able to sign the Declaration. Please remember that the signers were merely recognizing a fact that was already a reality.

In a book titled *The Sacred Rights of Conscience*, Professor Mark David Hall and his co-author Professor Daniel Dreisbach provide a plethora of evidence supporting the faith of the Founders and their intentions for the role of faith in our political system. They write:

> One of Congress's first acts was to agree to appoint and pay congressional chaplains. Shortly after doing so, it reauthorized the Northwest Ordinance, which held that 'Religion, morality, and knowledge being necessary to good government and the happiness of mankind, schools and the means of education shall forever be encouraged.'[16]

George Washington's Documented Words & Actions

As the American War for Independence began and George Washington was named Commander in Chief of the Continental Army, it soon became evident that the ill-equipped band of militias made up of farmers, local doctors, merchants, craftsmen, and members of local church congregations needed much discipline and training. Washington's first order of business was to implement strict rules of conduct for the army. The day after he took command, General Washington issued a general order for the army which stated that as commanding general, he required and expected each enlisted man to adhere to the rules or "articles of war" that he had established to govern his army. These rules included a provision that forbade cursing, profane language, and drunkenness. The rules went on to also require:

All Officers, and Soldiers, not engaged in actual duty, a

punctual attendance on Divine services, to implore the blessing of Heaven upon the means used for our safety and defence.[17]

This was not an exception to the rule, but the norm. How many times have you watched a special on the History Channel about America's War for Independence and heard things about these types of rules in Washington's army? Probably not too many.

Washington was in charge of a large and diverse group of enlisted men from all backgrounds, faith practices, and walks of life, and yet he understood that without what he called the intervention and blessing of Divine Providence, their efforts would be in vain. Humility, wisdom, understanding, and devotion were staples in his daily personal practice, and he held his men to those standards whenever possible.

Washington did this both on his own and with the support of the men who were serving in the Continental Congress. Representatives from all thirteen colonies continued to meet in Philadelphia, risking their lives and the lives of their families, in order to debate the merits and possibilities of independence from British rule. The session began with prayer and, regardless of their religious or philosophical differences, all took part in the solemn practice as they sought the wisdom and guidance of God together daily.

On July 20, 1776, in an act that is reminiscent of Gideon's six hundred men drinking water from the brook with one hand while holding weapons in the other, General Washington issued this order to his troops:

> The General orders this day (July 20, the first national fast day) to be religiously observed by the forces under his Command, exactly in manner directed by the Continental Congress. It is therefore strictly enjoined on all officers and soldiers to attend Divine service. And it is expected that all those who go to worship do take

their arms, ammunition and accouterments, and are prepared for immediate action, if called upon.[18]

The Black Robed Regiment

As the threat of war became imminent, many church ministers preached boldly from the pulpits, encouraging their congregations to pursue personal repentance before asking God to help them in the just and righteous cause of liberty. These bold and courageous preachers became known as the Black Robed Regiment. Their sermons were blatantly and unapologetically political, because their understanding of the natural rights of man was enlightened by their classical educations, their thorough knowledge of the Scriptures, and their understanding of this particular moment in history.

After studying the first Great Awakening and its far-reaching effect on American colonial culture, it is clear that the fruit of the revival was the realization of a personal relationship with God. This understanding brought with it the blessings of liberty mixed with individual accountability. Reverend William Gordon, pastor of the Third Church of Roxbury, preached a sermon to the Continental Congress before the national fast in 1775 and is recorded as saying,

> Our degeneracies, we must conclude from the light of nature and revelation, have contributed to bring us under the present calamities … We are now in an unusual way called upon to wash ourselves, to make ourselves clean, to put away the evil of our doings from before our eyes, to cease to do evil, to learn to do well, and to seek every kind of judgment.[19]

Many ministers and pastors, like Peter Muhlenberg of Pennsylvania, who pastored several frontier Lutheran congregations in Virginia and Pennsylvania, joined the Continental Army and personally enlisted full regiments from their congregations. It is historically recorded that after preaching a sermon on Ecclesiastes 3 and ending with verse 8, which reads, *"There is ... a time for war and a time for peace"* (KJV), Muhlenberg declared, "in the language of Holy write, there is a time to preach and a time to pray, but those times have passed away! There is a time to fight and that time is now!"[20] He gave the benediction and removed his clerical robes, revealing the full uniform of a colonel in the Continental Army. Coming down from the pulpit, he ordered the drums at the church door to beat for recruits. That day, Muhlenberg enlisted around three hundred men from his congregation and the local community, becoming the 8th Virginia Regiment. By the end of the war, Peter had been promoted to Brigadier General in charge of Washington's Light Infantry brigade.

As evidenced by letters between Peter and his brother Frederick Muhlenberg, who pastored a church in New York, Frederick did not approve of his brother's actions until he stood watching his own church being burned to the ground by the British. Frederick soon joined the fight as well and today, his portrait hangs in the Speaker's Lobby in the US Capitol in Washington, DC, where he is honored for his service as the first Speaker of the US House of Representatives.

As part of the National Statuary Hall Collection, each state in the union is allowed to display two statues of heroic citizens from their state in the US Capitol. It is a testament to the vision, service, and sacrifice of these two church clergymen and brothers, that one is pictured in a portrait, one of the largest in the Speaker's Lobby of the US Capitol, and the other, Peter, was chosen to be memorialized by the state of Pennsylvania with a marble statue of his likeness in the crypt of the US Capitol. I have had the privilege on many occasions to admire the portrait of Speaker Muhlenberg and to see the marble statue of his brother Peter in the crypt. I would encourage you to either visit the Capitol and see it in person or look them up online. Each time I see them, I am reminded of their courageous actions as men of faith, action, conviction, and courage.

"Give 'Em Watts, Boys!"

Another story of the Black Robed Regiment that has been all but lost to our history books is that of Reverend James Caldwell, known as "The Fighting Parson of the Revolution." In 1762, he was called to serve as pastor of the First Presbyterian Church in Elizabeth Town, NJ. He and his wife, Hannah, had nine children, and he was an early and active supporter of the War for Independence, joining the army as chaplain even before the Declaration of Independence was written. In his congregation was a signer of the Declaration of Independence, a later President of the Continental Congress, around forty officers of the colonial army, and many other patriots of historical action.

He preached regularly to the troops, served as commissary, and accepted no pay while living on the small stipend that his congregation could provide for his family. As the British became aware of his influence and reputation in the region, they put a price on his head. Hearing that the British would soon be coming through, and as documented by George Washington in a letter to Congress, Caldwell moved his family ten miles away out of safety concerns.

In 1777, Caldwell was given the title of Deputy Quarter Master. His duties included foraging and finding food, supplies, clothing, and weapons for the soldiers of his regiment. With no money and with great difficulty communicating or finding transportation while having a bounty on his head, he overcame great odds in finding supplies for the troops. One of the biggest challenges during the winter was finding shoes for the soldiers.

In 1779, a Hessian commander with five thousand troops was headed to Connecticut Farms, the town where Caldwell's family was staying. His wife believed that her presence would help prevent the pillaging and burning they had experienced in their hometown of Elizabeth Town. After providing refreshments to the enemy, somehow a member of the troop fired into the window of the room where Hannah was with the maid and the children, killing her instantly.

The people of the community were enraged. According to the story as recorded by the Union Township Historical Society in New Jersey:

James Caldwell had both his house and church burned by the British.

> While the Redcoats were retreating from the Battle of Connecticut Farms, a Loyalist spotted James' wife, Hannah, through a window and shot her dead in front of their children.
>
> From his pulpit and on horseback, he spread the word of her death. Hannah's sacrifice increased the determination of the Patriots to fight on for independence.[21]

Three weeks after the murder of his wife, on June 23, 1780, Reverend Caldwell helped the patriot troops defeat the British at the Battle of Springfield. During the battle, Caldwell realized that the men were quickly running out of wadding for their weapons. He ran to the Springfield Presbyterian Church, grabbed the Isaac Watts Hymn & Psalms hymn books, ran back to the soldiers, and started tearing out the pages for them to use. He proceeded to shout as he passed out the pages of the hymnals, "Now boys, give 'em Watts! Give 'em Watts!"[22]

Although the patriots were outnumbered and outgunned, they put up a valiant fight and were successful in stopping the enemy advance and preventing the enemy from capturing General Washington who was encamped not too far away at Morristown.

This is just a small sampling of the overwhelming body of evidence regarding the attitude that the founding generation had regarding the involvement of people of faith in political action. It is very different from the majority view today. The documentation is overwhelming and yet, as the spiritual descendants of these incredible people of faith, we have allowed ourselves to be duped into believing the lie that our founding was not based on Judeo-Christian principles.

Many Americans have accepted the lies being taught in our progressive, humanistic history books, so I have but I encourage you to take this little refresher course on the truth a refresher course on the truth from original documents and start your own research journey. If you do further research, you won't be disappointed!

The Practice of Faith in the American Colonies

As we study our history, it is important to keep in mind that the practice of Christianity in America in the late 1700s was quite different than it is today. Many Americans were not far removed from their grandparents or great-grandparents who had fled religious persecution in Europe, and many colonists were still struggling for religious freedom under the rule of the British governors.

A number of colonial legislatures had established an official government-sanctioned church and implemented taxation to sustain the official church of the colony. Those citizens who chose not to attend the approved church were still taxed and sometimes limited in their ability to participate in civic activities. Some were even imprisoned for their dissent. This had become a growing concern among the citizens in the years leading up to the War for Independence.

Another difference between today's Christianity and that of Colonial America is that the overwhelming majority (an estimated 98 percent) of Americans who practiced the Christian faith were well-educated in the Scriptures and many could read the original Biblical languages: Latin, Greek, and even Hebrew.

Education in the American Colonies

We often think of the colonists as the rejected poor and uneducated who had been chased from their homes across Europe, but nothing could be further from the truth. Many were people of means, title, and wealth. Many were descendants of nobility, well-educated, and extremely industrious. Classical education, which is making a huge comeback in America today, was the common educational experience of a large swath of home-educated colonists, and many sent their children to universities in Europe to finish their educations. The most common books found in the average household in the American colonies were the Bible and Blackstone's books on English Common Law. Children were educated at home, including lessons in the Bible, Latin, Greek, history, government, ancient literature, geometry, philosophy, elocution, penmanship, and much more.

One of countless examples of this higher level of home education is that of Major Benjamin Talmadge, Jr. of Long Island. During the War for Independence, in spite of the fact that he was in his early twenties, he served as General Washington's Chief of Intelligence and helped establish the famous Culper Spy Ring at Setauket, Long Island, which outwitted the British and helped win the war. To read Talmadge's life story, you might think he was a genius! He could read Latin at the age of eight and entered Yale at the age of fifteen, not because he didn't qualify to enter Yale earlier, but his father, a pastor on Long Island, who had homeschooled his children in the classical tradition, wanted Benjamin to be a little older before he enrolled. He was a close friend of patriot Nathan Hale's and was one of many students from Yale who had a deep dedication to the righteous cause of liberty and voluntarily entered Washington's army directly after college.

This story is just one example of the caliber and intellectual advancement that was common in early America. If you study the lives of Witherspoon, Madison, Adams, and others, you will be amazed at the intellectual prowess and philosophical depth that permeated American society.

A Deep Knowledge of the Nature of God

As a result of the incredible education of the majority of the colonial citizens, their understanding of the nature and characteristics of the God of Abraham, Isaac, and Jacob was incredibly deeper than the understanding claimed by the vast majority of American Christians today. They understood and recognized the laws of God and the order of His created world, and they had a clear view of their role in God's design.

The thorough knowledge of the attributes of the God of the Bible was reflected in their writings, prayers, and debates. In fact, George Washington used more than eighty names for God in his writings alone. He was not the exception, either. This use of descriptive terms for God and His character was common among the population of colonial America.

Some historians, in an attempt to downplay the role of faith in the founding of America, have criticized the many names of God used in early American documents. They have ignored the reverence that was shown for the many aspects of God's character. They claim that the references to God in our founding documents were purposefully "vague" and "veiled" in an attempt to be more "secular," or they claim that they were the result of the Deistic roots of the founders. Nothing could be further from the truth. If anything, the variety of descriptive references to God are proof of their deep understanding of God's nature and their desire to use the appropriate name for the attribute which best represented His character as they referred to Him in their writings.

George Washington kept a prayer journal for morning and evening prayers that is filled with evidence of his personal faith, his desire to be a better Christian, and admissions of his need for forgiveness and guidance. His prolific use of the various names of God reveals Washington's his deep understanding of Scripture. Here is just one example from his journal:

Almighty God, and most merciful father, who didst command the children of Israel to offer a daily sacrifice to thee, that thereby they might glorify and praise thee for thy protection both night and day, receive, O Lord, my morning sacrifice which I now offer up to thee; I yield thee humble and hearty thanks that thou has preserved me from the danger of the night past, and brought me to the light of the day, and the comforts thereof, a day which is consecrated to thine own service and for thine own honor. Let my heart, therefore, Gracious God, be so affected with the glory and majesty of it, that I may not do mine own works, but wait on thee, and discharge those weighty duties thou requirest of me, and since thou art a God of pure eyes, and wilt be sanctified in all who draw near unto thee, who doest not regard the sacrifice of fools, nor hear sinners who tread in thy courts, pardon, I beseech thee, my sins, remove them from thy presence, as far as the east is from the west, and accept of me for the merits of thy son Jesus Christ, that when I come into thy temple, and compass thine altar, my prayers may come before thee as incense; and as thou wouldst hear me calling upon thee in my prayers, so give me grace to hear thee calling on me in thy word, that it may be wisdom, righteousness, reconciliation and peace to the saving of the soul in the day of the Lord Jesus. Grant that I may hear it with reverence, receive it with meekness, mingle it with faith, and that it may accomplish in me, Gracious God, the good work for which thou has sent it. Bless my family, kindred, friends and country, be our God & guide this day and for ever for his sake, who lay down in the Grave and arose again for us, Jesus Christ our Lord, Amen.[23]

CHAPTER THREE

THE FAITH REQUIRED FOR SELF-GOVERNANCE

God and the US Constitution

Those who want to rewrite our history have pointed out the lack of reference to God in the Constitution. Let's be clear. Although the US Constitution does not use the same references to God that were so prominent in the Declaration of Independence— references such as "Divine Providence," "Creator," the "Supreme Judge of the World," or "Nature's God"—there is a very clear reason why such references were not used. In his article "Did America Have a Christian Founding?", written for the Heritage Foundation, Professor Mark Hall explains that the men who formed our government had agreed that the government would have a very limited purpose. They established that limited purpose for the new government in Article 1, Section 8 of the US Constitution. Hall explains:

> There was almost universal agreement that if there was to be legislation on religious or moral matters, it should be done by state and local governments. In fact, states remained active in this business well into the 20th century. ... The First Amendment merely reinforced this understanding with respect to the faith—i.e., *Congress*

has no power to establish a national church or restrict the free exercise of religion.[24]

In 1832, the last official state church in America was rescinded or disestablished, but even then, many states still retained laws that required candidates for public office to pass certain religious criteria. Well into the early 1900s, many states also kept laws in place which required prayer and Bible reading in schools. They did so because it was within their jurisdiction, according to the US Constitution, which limited the federal government from addressing such issues. Both levels of government stayed within their respective bounds and limitations until the late nineteenth century.

The Declaration of Independence had made the sacred and divine case to the world for separation from Britain, based on the fact that we are "endowed by our Creator with certain unalienable rights."[25] The next step in forming a federal government was to write a constitution. It outlined the parameters of the new government and had a particular emphasis on the limitations of that government. Therefore, there was no need to address a subject such as religion, other than in the First Amendment, ensuring that the federal government would not have the ability to establish a government-sanctioned church. The debate between the limitations of the powers of the federal government and the rights and jurisdictions of the state governments was a theme of ongoing debate back then, and it continues today.

Hall and Dreisbach, in *Sacred Rights of Conscience*, provide insight into the mindsets of the founders as well as detailed documentation of their actions, as further evidence. They provide historic documents revealing that the actions of the founders who wrote the First Amendment clearly express their support for elected officials taking part in religious expression. They did not view it as a governmental approval of any particular religion, but as an act of free men, duly elected representatives of the people, expressing their personal beliefs in a public way and encouraging the same freedom of expression by the citizens.

The day after the House of Representatives approved the final wording of the Bill of Rights, on September 25, 1789, Elias Boudinot, who served as the president of the American Bible Society, authored a resolution asking that there be a day of Thanksgiving officially observed by the nation. He proposed that President Washington should "recommend a day of public thanksgiving and prayer to be observed by acknowledging, with grateful hearts, the many signal favors of Almighty God, especially by affording them an opportunity peaceably to establish a Constitution of government for their safety and happiness."[26] Some of the members objected, fearing that such a "recommendation" from the President would remind the people of the religious edicts of European rulers. Some objected because they believed that it was not the jurisdiction of the federal government but should be left to the individual states.

The great Roger Sherman spoke in support of the proposal. He spoke eloquently that the recommendation was not equivalent to an edict, and that at times of significant and obvious blessing from heaven, the the Bible gave the precedent for such a recommendation to be given by the President. Sherman is recorded by a newspaper of the era as saying the proposal was:

> Warranted by a number of precedents in holy writ: for instance, the solemn thanksgivings and rejoicings which took place in the time of Solomon, after the building of the temple, was a case in point. This example, he thought, worthy of Christian imitation on the present occasion; and he would agree with the gentleman who moved the resolution.[27]

After the debate on the proposal, the House voted to pass the measure, and it was also passed by the Senate. The President approved as well, and the result was George Washington's 1789 Thanksgiving Day Proclamation.[28]

Hall clarifies further in "Did America Have a Christian Founding?" that it was not the will of the founders to establish an official government sanctioned church like those in Europe, and the majority of them opposed any such established church on the state level as well. This did not deter them from speaking about their faith or allowing the government to proclaim recommendations for the people to honor God in their own way. There was strong agreement that both state and federal officials and elected public servants were permitted and even encouraged to speak of their faith publicly and to make religious arguments in the public arena. Religion was to be part of the public debate and a vital part of the national identity. Hall concludes:

> There was virtually no support for contemporary visions of a separation of church and state that would have political leaders avoid religious language and require public spaces to be stripped of religious symbols.[29]

The One Assumption the Founders Made

We must note that in order to ensure the preservation of our liberties, the Founders made one assumption: *the continued engagement of a moral citizenry*. In a letter to the Massachusetts Militia in October of 1798, President John Adams wrote:

> Our Constitution was made only for a moral and religious People. It is wholly inadequate to the government of any other.[30]

This was the belief that permeated the Constitutional Convention as the elected delegates from the thirteen colonies came together to form a new government. James Madison spent many months preceding the convention, studying the failures and triumphs of governments throughout history. Reading books in at least four different languages and having a deep understanding of the greatest legal and philosophical minds of ancient Greece, Rome, and England, Madison arrived at the convention with a fully completed and thorough proposal that would form the basis of the debates.

The underlying assumption of each member of the convention was that whatever form of government was formed, it would be reliant on one mitigating factor for its success or failure: the continuing dedication of the citizens to the moral principles of the Bible and a Judeo-Christian worldview. The American culture had already been established for a century or more in America. Their goal was to give the people the tools to continue to grow the blessings of liberty by engaging in a lively and morally sound system of natural rights and Providential order.

A Maryland delegate to the Constitutional Convention, James McHenry, kept a journal. On the last day of the conventions, September 18, 1787, he records that Benjamin Franklin was greeted by a woman named Elizabeth Willing Powell outside the Constitutional Convention. She asked what type of government the convention had given the American people. McHenry records that Benjamin Franklin famously replied, "A Republic, if you can keep it."[31]

In a letter to his wife Abigail, on the passage of the Declaration of Independence on July 2, 1776, John Adams wrote:

> I am apt to believe that it will be celebrated, by succeeding Generations, as the great anniversary Festival. It ought to be commemorated, as the Day of Deliverance by solemn Acts of Devotion to God Almighty. It ought to be solemnized with Pomp and Parade, with Shews, Games, Sports, Guns, Bells, Bonfires and Illuminations

from one End of this Continent to the other from this Time forward forever more.

You will think me transported with Enthusiasm but I am not. — I am well aware of the Toil and Blood and Treasure, that it will cost Us to maintain this Declaration, and support and defend these States. — Yet through all the Gloom I can see the Rays of ravishing Light and Glory. I can see that the End is more than worth all the Means. And that Posterity will tryumph in that Days Transaction, even altho We should rue it, which I trust in God We shall not.[32]

Another Founding Father and first Justice of the Supreme Court, John Jay, wrote, "We must go home to be happy, and our home is not in this world. Here we have nothing to do but our duty."[33]

But perhaps the words inscribed on the grave of Governor William Bradford of Plymouth Colony, more than a century before the Declaration of Independence was signed, give the most poignant warning for Americans today: "What our fathers with so much difficulty attained, do not basely relinquish."

The Privilege of Self-Governance

Let's be clear: the original definition of civic duty meant far more to that first generation of Americans than merely voting in a presidential election every four years. After risking everything against the greatest army in the world for a chance at self-governance and true liberty, the first generation of Americans knew firsthand the cost of freedom. They cherished their right to read proposed ordinances, attend public hearings and speeches, read campaign materials, and to determine for themselves the direction of their nation. Thousands turned out for public debates between candidates. They were constantly following every decision that their elected officials made. They attended congressional debates, court hearings, and town halls. They read reports in newspapers and periodicals, and they were active in all aspects of society.

At the end of the war in Afghanistan, I remember seeing the joy and exhilaration on the faces of those first Afghans who took part in the first elections and dipped their fingers in purple ink to show that they had voted. That should have been a poignant reminder to us that being allowed to choose our leaders is a rare and precious privilege which the majority of the world does not possess.

Understanding the true stories of those who came to American shores in search of freedom a century before the war with Britain also helps our understanding of what our "engagement" as citizens and as Christians was originally intended to be. It means more than casting a vote every four years.

As Thomas Paine described it in his popular pamphlet, *Common Sense,*

> This new World hath been the asylum for the persecuted lovers of civil and religious liberty from every part of Europe. Hither have they fled, not from the tender embraces of the mother, but from the cruelty of the monster; and it is so far true of England, that the same tyranny which drove the first emigrants from home, pursues their descendants still.[34]

From the sacrifices of the first settlers seeking religious freedom to the preaching of George Whitefield and the first Great Awakening revivals on the American continent before the break with Britain, to John Adams' references to faith in God and his commitment to Scripture in his many speeches and writings, to James Madison and George Mason's work on the Bill of Rights during the Constitutional Convention, to Washington's letter to the Touro Synagogue in Rhode Island, to John Jay and Alexander Hamilton's society for the abolition of slavery in New York City, our Founding Fathers took painstaking care to ensure that our natural rights would be preserved in a way that would allow for the free exercise of conscience. They did so while safeguarding us from persecution by prohibiting the federal or state government from establishing any kind of state-sanctioned church.

The Tools They Left Behind

How did they do all of this? By entrusting every American citizen with a governmental system which provided the means by which to continually preserve our own liberties, if we would do our part to be informed and involved.

The biblical verses engraved in stone and marble on our government buildings and monuments in Washington, DC, as well as in every state capitol in the nation, were placed there as permanent reminders of the Judeo-Christian virtues that were woven into the fabric of every aspect of our government and culture. It was no accident. It was an act of faith and hope by our founders—faith and hope in us, their descendants. It was a permanent testimony to the fact that the Bible and Divine Providence had been a guiding light to those who paved the way for us. The Scripture engraved in stone was also put there in case the basis of our founding was ever brought into question, and over the past fifty years or more, that is exactly what has happened.

The Bible teaches us, *"For unto whomsoever much is given, of him shall much be required; and to whom men have committed much, of him they will ask the more"* (Luke 12:21, KJV).

In an article for the Family Research Council in 2018, titled "For Christians, Voting Is Not an Option. It Is a Divine Calling," Patrina Mosely and David Closson wrote:

> In the context of American politics, voting is a practical application of a biblical worldview … In America, because ultimate sovereignty resides with the people,

voting is essentially the delegation of authority. For Christians, this means suffrage (voting) is inherently a matter of stewardship.[35]

Comparisons to Pre-World War II Germany

Some say that the American church today is facing the same challenge as that of the German church in the years leading up to World War II. They warn that people of faith in America should be vigilant and bold to speak the truth and protect the innocent and the weak from being stripped of their God-given rights. I agree with the warning, but I would argue that there is a poignant difference between the American church today and that of the German church before World War II.

Because of the critical role that people of faith played in forming the American government, I believe that the American church is actually ten times more responsible for the state of American governance than the German church was at that time.

Those devout believers who studiously and faithfully debated, discussed, articulated, and sacrificed to establish our unique form of government fought to ensure that the opportunity and responsibility of governance would be placed squarely on the shoulders of every citizen for every generation. Each generation of Americans has had a chance to hold positions in government, be involved in the process, preserve the truth of our founding principles, stand up against oppression and abuse, and make a difference for freedom around the world. More than any other nation, we have been given a form of government which allows each generation of Americans the chance to defend and preserve their own freedoms by voting to elect our rulers and even running for office in an effort to right societal wrongs and serve our fellow citizens.

The framers put the power in the hands of the people and ignited the fire of liberty in the hearts of all Americans, inspiring them to not only preserve and defend the freedoms of American citizens, but also to eventually be willing to fight for the liberation of millions around the globe. My Israeli guide was right. With the power of the unique American culture, government, and a purposed return to our founding principles, America can continue to be a light to the world.

CHAPTER FOUR

"I DON'T DO POLITICS."

"The only foundation for ... a republic is to be laid
in Religion. Without this there can be no virtue, and
without virtue there can be no liberty, and liberty is
the object and life of all republican governments."

Dr. Benjamin Rush

<small>SIGNER OF THE DECLARATION OF INDEPENDENCE[36]</small>

The soft-spoken, thirty-something lady was a member of a growing church in our community. She was describing a scene to me that sounded all too familiar, and as she told her story, I could picture it in my mind. The buzzing sound of people chatting, laughing, and greeting each other at church would be followed by announcements, then congregational singing, a Scripture reading, and a sermon. It was a local church body like so many countless thousands that have existed across the landscape of America, dating back to before we were a nation.

This sweet young mother was just like most of us: busy with life and a never-ending list of things to do each day. You know the routine. Days usually begin with getting the kids up, dressed, fed and off to school, then heading to work. Going to evening ball games, dance class, or school activities was probably her routine on a weeknight, followed by either a fast food dinner with the team or a stop at the grandparents' house for a home-cooked meal. Once home, it was time for homework, chores, showers, and hopefully a time of prayer before getting the kids in bed. After that, maybe she would have time to work on finances, watch some local news, or make plans for the next vacation before heading off to bed to face another day.

She knew I had been active in politics for many years, so she looked up with a bit of a strange expression, almost perplexed, and prefaced her question by letting me know how thankful she was for the abundant blessings that God had poured out on America. Then, because I "was in politics" she awkwardly said, "I don't know how to say this, but for some reason it bothered me that my pastor mentioned the upcoming election this past week in his sermon—from the pulpit. He mentioned something about a Voter Guide too. I mean, wasn't that unconstitutional?"

"Unconstitutional?" I asked.

"Well, I am totally for Christians being involved in government and all, but a pastor talking about it from the pulpit just didn't seem right. Doesn't that go against our separation of church and state law?"

"The church and state law?" I asked, knowingly.

"In the Constitution!" she quipped, as if she were shocked by my ignorant question. "I'm not an expert, and I really don't do politics, but that's pretty basic to our democracy, isn't it?"

"Before I answer, let me ask you something, just out of curiosity. Did you vote in the primary election in May?"

"The primary? I don't think so. Was that for president?"

Remembering how I had needed a refresher course in civics back when I began to get involved in politics, I explained, "Well, it was an election to make your choice from the candidates in your political party for president and for other offices down the ballot as well."

"Oh. I don't think I did. I don't like either party, anyway," she replied. "They all pretty much seem the same to me. And the commercials are awful, aren't they? I don't see how you can stand it!"

She laughed nervously. I truly wanted to put her at ease, and so I let her know that she was definitely not alone in her observation.

"Yes, political commercials can be a little much. But back to your question. Are you wanting my opinion on church leaders encouraging their members to take part in elections?"

"Well, yes. I mean, I know we should all vote, but to say that from the pulpit just rubs me wrong, It seems like it goes against our founding principles, doesn't it?" she asked, with a little glint of doubt in her eyes.

Unfortunately, this was not the first time I had heard these sentiments from a practicing Christian American, and I'm sure you can guess how the rest of the conversation went. I shared my usual explanation with her as kindly as possible. No, there is not a "separation of church and state clause" in the US Constitution, but there is a prohibition on the "establishment of religion" by the government which is found in the Bill of Rights. Yes, it is completely acceptable, and in fact there is an historic tradition for American pastors and church leaders to speak boldly from the pulpit regarding political matters. I shared the amazing stories involving America's Black Robed Regiment comprised of church leaders from all denominations in all thirteen colonies, who not only preached but recruited and led full regiments of soldiers from their congregations to fight in America's War for Independence.

I reminded her of the many concerns she had shared in the past regarding school curriculums, freedom of speech issues, the limitations on our right to bear arms, and so many other issues that affect us on a daily basis. It just took a little discussion and a few factual reminders for her to understand the importance of what her pastor had done and the established precedent he was following by doing so.

The Present State of American Politics

We have all felt disdain and even disgust for the current political landscape in America, and we might have even uttered the words, "I don't do politics" or something similar at some point in our lives. The state of corruption, greed, hunger for power, and a desire for control over the lives of others in our current system stands in stark contrast to the humble, servant-hearted leadership and sacrificial example we find in the life of Christ. Why would we ever want to be a part of something that is so diametrically opposed to the biblical principles He taught, such as loving our neighbor or being kind to one another or the last shall be first?

I think the following quote by Adams is almost prophetic when you look at our current political landscape today. In a letter to James Warren on April 22, 1776, Adams wrote:

> I fear that in every elected office, members will obtain an influence by noise, not sense. By meanness, not greatness. By ignorance, not learning. By contracted hearts, not large souls ... There must be decency and respect.[37]

Do some of our elected officials obtain "influence by noise?" I think so. Are the House and Senate marked by "meanness," division, and conflict? Most definitely, yes. Think of the billions of dollars that are spent on political campaigns each election cycle. How many divisive ads bombard your eyes and ears on television, social media, and radio? How much dis-information and outright lies have been spread either out of ignorance or purposefully by the media or by those in office who desire to garner headlines? The list would be endless! It is hard to decipher fact from fiction anymore!

Does it seem like all of the sensational claims, manipulative language, efforts to create class envy, outrageous promises, and over-the-top marketing gimmicks from candidates today should *not* be the basis on which we elect our leaders? I wholeheartedly agree. Have you noticed the trend of candidates spending exorbitant amounts of money which they raise from big lobbyists and special interest groups in order to run successful political campaigns? If not, please pay attention!

Special interest groups and DC-funded dark money campaigns "leak" false articles to the media in an effort to slander candidates who they see as posing a threat to the political system. The federal bureaucracies pick winners and losers in business and in politics in a variety of ways, and those with investigative power use that power to target law-abiding citizens. The list of pet projects and priorities that big money groups demand of political leadership is long and exorbitant. Pay to play and political favors are commonplace. It is sad, but those elected leaders who dare to follow their conscience are targeted by well-funded groups with large memberships who want to hold their financial "sword of Damocles" over those who are supposed to be representing the people.

Frankly, the whole system can be just plain ugly and sometimes even repugnant to people of deep faith. As we stand back in disbelief at our current political landscape, it seems easier to walk away, wrap our self-righteous robes around us, and pray for the Lord's quick return. Yet, as harsh as this may seem, as Americans, we only need to look in the mirror to know who is to blame.

A Long Look in the Mirror

As people who believe and try to follow the Bible, the question we must ask is: Have we not been have we not been guilty of similar behavior on a smaller scale? Are there not politics in the church? Have you ever seen a church member threaten to withdraw their membership or withhold their donation if a certain action was not taken in the church? In the church, is there not a tendency toward elevating those who have been successful in business or who contribute large amounts to the church building fund to positions of leadership, not based on their spiritual testimony and consistent walk of faith, but simply based on the fact that they are financially successful and therefore must be a person of wisdom? Many times they are very wise, but there are times when a smart businessman or woman might not make the right kind of church leader.

As a Christian who has been active in the church and involved in American government in different ways for two decades, it is clear to me that our political system is merely an exaggerated reflection of what we have allowed in the church. We have even allowed a certain amount of internal politics to creep into our businesses and other local organizations. When we allow corruption to be tolerated or hidden, even in the smallest ways, it is only a matter of time before we do the same in selecting our political leaders. The church is meant to lead, but when we see corruption in our American government, and we realize that our elected leaders are a reflection of the people, we must conclude one of two things: The people have tolerated corruption, or the people have neglected to elect moral leaders.

How can we hold our elected leaders accountable, when we do not hold our church members or business partners accountable? How can we lead when we are so eagerly trying to follow movie stars or sports figures or the wealthy moguls of Wall Street or the political leaders in Washington? With an estimated 384,000 churches in America, there is no excuse. If we see corruption in our culture, then we need to look in the mirror and examine our own hearts. People of faith must lead by example and by action first in order to change the course of our nation. When we hold one another accountable to the guidelines of biblical morality, we will do the same in the public arena. After all, we do have a representative form of government.

President James A. Garfield was also a congressman and a minister of the Gospel. During America's centennial year, he wrote in an article for the *Atlantic Monthly*:

The people are responsible for the character of their Congress. If that body be ignorant, reckless, and corrupt, it is because the people tolerate ignorance, recklessness, and corruption … If the next centennial does not find us a great nation … it will be because those who represent the enterprise, the culture, and the morality of the nation do not aid in controlling the political forces.[38]

It is when we fill our lives with so many seemingly important activities, commitments, and obligations that we can easily find ourselves neglecting our basic responsibilities as American citizens which make all of our activities even possible. I have seen it played out many times. When people of faith either seclude or bury themselves in their own circles of activity, and neglect civic engagement, soon the absence of the kindness, compassion, reason, and lasting solutions they would bring to the public discourse is felt by society as a whole. Our absence and disengagement brings with them dire consequences.

The Reagan Doctrine

Keep in mind that those who seek public office will not do it perfectly. President Ronald Reagan said that he was happy if he could agree with someone on eighty percent of the issues and he viewed them as a friend and ally, "not a twenty percent traitor." I encourage you to make a list of issues that are non-negotiable to you. There are moral absolutes that cannot be compromised, therefore you should base your support for political candidates on those who agree with you on those issues.

In government, there are issues that are not moral absolutes, like the amount of road funding that is needed in a county or the expansion of an intersection. Local, state, and national governments have many different areas of responsibility, and there are many different ways to address issues. If your elected official casts a vote with which you disagree on an issue that is negotiable, find a gracious way to agree to disagree. My great-grandmother used to say, "The arm of flesh will fail you." She meant that we are all human and we should not demand perfection from one another because we will all fail at some point. That is human nature.

The benefit of electing leaders who follow God and hold our same worldview is that they have an underlying moral compass which provides spiritual discernment and clarity on challenging issues. This clarity of moral purpose will guide them on the non-negotiable issues and will always inspire them to serve the people first and foremost.

Have you ever heard someone say, "You can't legislate morality"? I think what they are trying to say is that you can't force people to do the right thing. That is true, but there is an aspect of the statement we need to re-think. Laws are crafted by humans. Every human has their own worldview and value system. If their bill is trying to increase the penalty for domestic violence convictions, it is probably because they believe that domestic violence is wrong and should be punished more severely. They are legislating based on a set of moral principles. They are legislating their own morality, based on their assessment of right and wrong. This is why it is so important to vet candidates before they are elected. We will discuss this in detail in a later chapter.

It is time we realize that people of faith are the anchor securing our ship of state.

The Dilemma of Political Parties

In his farewell address to the nation, President Washington gave a dire warning about the "spirit of party" as he called it. He warned of the divisiveness and factions that come from political parties.[39] He was very right about all of it, and yet over time, in an effort to define the difference in candidates, political parties began to form in America. From the Whigs and the Democrats to the Republicans and Libertarians, we have had our share of platforms and parties! People of faith are guided by their moral principles and the natural laws of God, and that is why it is important not just to know where the political parties stand on issues, but where individual candidates stand. We will discuss how to vet candidates in a later chapter because there is more to it than just the letter behind their name. Regardless of the political system, we can still navigate our way to finding and supporting a candidate who will best represent our values.

Some have referred to the polarization of our culture as a by-product of the slow decline in morals and our tribal nature as humans. They rightly decry blind loyalty to political parties and plead with the church to be committed purely to the practice of faith, not the tribe of political parties. It is true that our loyalty should be to God first and foremost, but I believe that as Americans, that loyalty to God should inspire us to be people of action, applying biblical principles to our decisions in choosing our leaders. Even if we do not like the party system, the reality is that we have to work within the existing framework of our political system as it is. This includes our willingness to hold political office in order to safeguard our freedoms, and in the current system, that requires choosing a party affiliation when you become a candidate. Please take the time to browse through excerpts from the major party platforms at the back of this book and follow the links provided to read all of the political platforms.

Your Faith Will Guide You

I want to emphasize that if you run for office, or decide to get involved with your local party, it is not a choice of faith over party, and it should never be. Our faith should inform our decision in supporting a candidate and a political party. As Lord John Acton clearly states in his many writings on liberty and faith, we are obligated by the very nature of our form of government to act in both realms.

Lord Acton has been called the "magistrate of history" and was widely respected as one of the greatest historians of freedom in the 19th century. In his 1877 address entitled "The History of Freedom in Antiquity," he stated, "Liberty is the essential condition and guardian of religion."[40] How profoundly true! Without freedom, we are limited in our ability to speak freely, to practice our faith, or to reach the world with the light of God. If we do not stand in the public arena while we have the freedom to do so, our ability to be active on both fronts—both spiritual and political—will soon be in jeopardy. As we look at our nation today, it is clear that the long absence of Christians and people of faith in positions of leadership is beginning to reap a harvest of dire consequences.

Hesitance and Hope

I am not suggesting that people of faith have been completely absent. I know many elected officials personally who have served in the public arena and have the scars to prove it. But the increasing trend among Bible believing people of faith in America who profess to believe the Bible to withdraw from politics is very real.

The majority will vote in general elections, if not the primary, and try to vote their conscience, but after hearing from literally hundreds of voters in small towns and big cities over the years, the general consensus is that the ugliness and convoluted corruption that has grown greater with each election cycle seems a little too overwhelming for them to risk too much involvement. Many have asked the question, "Why would any 'good' person want to risk their reputation and put their family through such a divisive process?" It's a valid concern. With so many different responsibilities in life, from our work to our children, to our community and church activities, it is hard to find the bandwidth for anything else, much less contemplate being involved in the mudslinging campaigns we see on television.

The good news is that all of that ugliness is not the actual reality of grassroots politics in America, at least not yet. Local politics is usually friendly, community members who support each other and work together to provide needed solutions for their friends and neighbors. I have experienced this and seen it played out in my little corner of America, and I hope that it serves to encourage your heart as it has mine. As we will soon explore, engagement in local politics is not as intimidating or demanding as it seems, and the majority of it is not ugly, either. As with anything, there are exceptions. If you try, you will be pleasantly surprised by how easy it is to be engaged in your community, and it is that engagement that is exactly what will make the difference in saving America.

Before we get into the details of how to be engaged, we need to recognize a unique challenge that is facing our generation.

Access to Information and Misinformation

A shift is occurring that has been expedited in its speed by the fever pitch of information coming at us from the huge number of new media outlets and all the competitive marketing gimmicks that bombard us on a daily basis. This flood of information and misinformation raises a new challenge for the average American. As we learn to filter through the noise and find the truth, we also face the challenge of dealing with a large swath of the population who believe the humanist, Marxist philosophies which have been taught in our schools and universities for the past century.

Our challenge in this generation is twofold:

1. To remind ourselves of the true foundations of our government in order to combat the misinformation.
2. To overcome the noise of misinformation and find effective ways to be engaged in returning the government and the culture to its founding principles.

This major shift in our culture came after decades of moral and spiritual decline and after a humanist philosophy (which we will discuss in detail later) became accepted into the mainstream of our society. The removal of prayer and Bible reading from public schools, the introduction of evolutionary theory as scientific fact, the rejection of the nuclear family, the acceptance of abortion on demand, and so many more shifts in the moral fabric of our nation came as a result of a subtle movement by humanistic philosophers to elevate man's intellect and scientific advancements over faith in the Creator God.

Research expert and prolific faith and culture author George Barna writes about the rapid decline of our American culture and presents some strategies that might bring our nation back to our foundations in his book *The Seven Faith Tribes*. [41] In an article discussing the book titled, "America's Seven Faith Tribes Hold the Key to National Restoration," Barna cites results from his analysis of over 30,000 interviews with Americans. He cites statistics that predict the demise of fundamental institutions which have been the key to our national strength: families, schools, the media, churches, and government.

From the research, it is clear that Americans have lost their motivation to work, due to government entitlement programs. That shift has changed attitudes from self-reliance to self-indulgence, expecting personal needs to be met by the market and even customized for us. The entitlement mentality is rampant in our culture. This idea, that a person is entitled to certain provisions by our government and even by the marketplace, has wreaked havoc on the free market and has had a negative influence on our churches as well. Some question whether the free market is even able to continue. We have been fed so much misinformation about the role of government, the role of faith, and the role of citizens, that it is hard to understand how far we have drifted from our original purpose.

The Church Must Lead

Barna's article made a poignant observation in pointing to the fact that the church in America has emulated the competitive nature of the business world and has started to focus more on counting members and money instead of morals and ministry. If we are honest with ourselves, we know that there is truth to this observation, especially in the American church.

Churches add extra programs, elaborate stages, and impressive talent trying to attract larger crowds. This has led to the neglect of teaching the foundational truths for which people are truly searching: responsibility to God, the infallibility of Scripture, service to others, compassion, a higher purpose, simple faith, the importance of family, the joy of obedience, holding each other accountable in love, and other timeless principles found in the Bible.[42]

This research should be a wakeup call to all Americans. Instead of the church and people of faith leading the nation by example and by being actively involved in every aspect of choosing our political leaders, we have lost our bearing, done the minimal amount of civic duty, failed to research candidates, and found ourselves too busy to keep tabs on those we elect.

From the beginning, God established three institutions: the family, the government, and the church. Much like a three-legged stool, when one leg is out of balance, the entire stool is unsteady and becomes useless. The church is tasked with teaching God's truth boldly, holding believers accountable, and ministering to those in need in the community they serve. But when the church fails in these areas, it has proven true that the government is all too eager to swoop in and fill the role of instructor and caregiver.

The problem is that the government was not meant to do these things and utterly fails in its attempt. Slowly, the church's role of ministering to the poor, the widows, the orphans, and the neglected has been abdicated to the government, and this has wreaked havoc on our families, communities, and morals. We have watched the astronomical increase of single parent homes and witnessed the growing trend of aging seniors becoming more and more reliant on government money.

By following instead of leading, people of faith have slowly weakened our influence in society, resulting in a drastic lowering of moral standards in our elected officials. We should not be surprised that our national unity is splintered when the church is following the competitive, individualistic model of Wall Street. Adopting a mindset that is so diametrically opposed to our values can only end in confusion and ineffectiveness. There should be a stark contrast in the way we order our lives, the way we follow our calling, the way we worship, and the way we spread God's light in our communities. It is that living contrast that will eventually bring those who are truly seeking peace into the light of God's truth.

Education by Soundbites and Podcasts

With the advent of easy access to new platforms for public dialogue, combined with the anonymity and lack of accountability for those who engage in it, the level of misinformation we see on a daily basis is astounding. Add to that the rise of AI, and I believe it will get worse before it gets better. It's also concerning that so few people take the time to truly research anything anymore. With this new generation of digital natives, a YouTube video can easily supersede the study of original sources.

For example, I remember attending an event where American history was being taught, and during the presentation, an acquaintance of mine who is in the Millennial generation heard the name George Washington mentioned. Immediately after the presentation, she wanted to share her "knowledge" about his life with me. She proceeded to go on a rant about how terrible the man was in every way. He "lied to Congress!" she said. He "stole money from the people by never paying the money he owed to Congress." He "left his wife all the time." His whole life was a "sham" and he "definitely wasn't a good General or even a good Christian." I was completely speechless.

After she was done, the only thing I could think to say was, "Wow! Where did you learn all that?" She said she listened to a certain podcast about the "true history" of America and gave me the title and author. A podcast! I was in such shock after her bold and over-confident diatribe that, instead of trying to argue with her, which would have been utterly pointless in the situation, I told her I would look up the podcast.

Upon further investigation, I found that the podcast had come under heavy fire from a long list of respected American historians for its failure to present facts or documented evidence regarding its content. It was so full of false information that the series on American presidents had been discontinued after a very short time. The author had been discredited and had moved on to some other way of spreading her political agenda to unsuspecting readers or listeners. And yet, the young person who had listened to it now considered herself "informed" about the truth regarding the Father of our Nation. Wow!

Please be careful with the sources you trust and where you get your information! We must be diligent to make sure that our sources are documented, credible, and accurate, and we must teach our children to do the same. In a later chapter, I will give you a list of reliable sources that have been consistent in their presentation of documented facts and accurate information. It does take extra time, but if you are concerned about the future of America, I implore you to take advantage of the resources provided in this book. I encourage you to take it further in your own journey by studying original sources and documents referenced in the end notes of this book as well.

Recognizing What Unites Us

Another part of the unique challenge we face in this new digital age is that we must guard against the tendency to jump into arguments on social media. Let's remind ourselves that we agree with our friends and neighbors on the vast majority of issues most of the time. With the astronomical growth of the internet in the past three decades, the rise of the twenty-four-hour news cycle, the increasing sensationalism of the entertainment industry, and constant bombardment of misinformation from social media, is it any wonder that the American people have been polarized and divided? Is it any wonder that we mistrust each other so much?

We have our pick of information sources—a smorgasbord of content that we can handpick according to what we want to hear and who we want to trust. Add to that equation the increasing absence of people of faith from the public square, whether in media, politics, or otherwise—people who should be sharing the truth in love, articulating fact-based reason, and offering constructive dialogue to our political discourse—and the problems in our culture are just compounded. We must do our research, arm ourselves with truth, and re-engage with confident kindness! Be encouraged that the answer is within reach. It starts with those who have faith in God individually deciding to make time to pray, study, and do more than just vote.

To Faith Leaders

If you are a church leader, you have a great responsibility to teach, develop, and foster a spiritual awakening in the hearts of those whom you lead. The spirit of kindness, hospitality, friendship, and compassion will only multiply as it is shared. I firmly believe that with diligent effort, the moral decay of our national character can be reversed. It won't happen with one election, and it won't even happen in two, but I pray we will have the moral courage to look in the mirror and agree with God that it must begin with us. It must begin with our families, our churches, and our communities.

One by one, as faith-filled leaders offer themselves as public servants, or preach boldly from the pulpit against corruption, soon you will see a different culture beginning to emerge. It might be difficult and even scary at times because of our learned divisions and the misguided polarization that exists. You might even face threats and persecution from authorities who adhere to the socialist approach to governing they were taught in school. That's why it is important to know your rights and be ready with an answer.

Recognize and acknowledge to your congregation that there is a true enemy at work, seeking to destroy the bedrock principles which made our nation great. It is undeniably at work in our culture more than ever before, but it is helpful when leaders call it out boldly. We send missionaries around the world to help those in need, to share the light of God, and I believe that we must view our beloved nation as a mission field as well. We see evil all around us in violent riots, mass shootings, flagrant disregard for authority, and the complete rejection of God's natural order. Drug addiction is on the rise. Anger, confusion, rebellion, and hopelessness are like plagues among our young people. We need leaders to stand boldly, confidently, and compassionately to speak truth and lead the way. If we actively engage in our culture, very soon we will see our school board or county council will be led by people of faith who live what they preach and are held accountable by their friends and neighbors. That engagement and diligent effort will begin to have a huge impact on cleaning up corruption in our communities, in our states, and eventually across the nation.

The questions we must ask ourselves are these:

1. Have we been so busy with our lives or even been consumed with being a light to the rest of the world that we have taken our American liberty for granted? Has our security lulled us into apathy?

2. Have we relinquished our duty and given it to those who have used it for the wrong purposes?
3. Have we gotten so caught up in debating total strangers on social media that we have forgotten to take action in the real world?

It is time to check our spiritual and political temperature and be open to an honest assessment of our role in the moral decline of our nation. I would highly recommend that you do a search online for a free book by Noah Webster, titled *Instructive and Entertaining Lessons for Youth: With Rules for Reading and Propriety.* The wisdom contained in it is priceless and timeless, and as I read through his pages of advice, I found it completely applicable even today. Webster also shared his insight regarding our responsibilities as citizens in his *History of the United States* (1832):

> If the citizens neglect their Duty and place unprincipled men in office, the government will soon be corrupted; laws will be made, not for the public good so much as for selfish or local purposes; corrupt or incompetent men will be appointed to execute the Laws; the public revenues will be squandered on unworthy men; and the rights of the citizen will be violated or disregarded ... If a republican government fails to secure public prosperity and happiness, it must be because the citizens neglect the Divine commands, and elect bad men to make and administer the laws.[43]

So you don't do politics? Beware. Someone else will take the opportunity to do it for you, and you might not like the outcome.

CHAPTER FIVE

WHO DETERMINES AMERICAN CULTURE?

I am going to reveal something that has taken me over fifteen years of engagement in both state and federal government to realize. If you learn nothing else from this book, please remember this:

Politics is always downwind of culture, and in America, our culture rises and falls on the leadership or failure of the church and people of faith.

As the culture goes, so goes the government and, eventually, so goes policy that affects our children, our churches, our schools, and even our armed forces. To be completely blunt, the literal front lines in the battle for America can be found in our homes, our families, our communities, and our churches. It starts with "We the people."

If Americans are honest with themselves, they will have to admit that the elected leaders in our state houses and in Congress are only a reflection of the culture at large. They are a reflection of us, and it would be wise to take a long, hard look in our political mirror! There have been many surveys and polls taken regarding how voters view Congress, and the results are always the same. The approval rating for Congress is always abysmal!

However, the interesting part of many of these polls is that most Americans think that their own member of Congress is great! It's "all the other members of Congress" who are the problem.

For the most part, we elect those whom we believe best represent our values and share our worldview, so whether we like it or not, our elected leaders reflect our own culture, virtues, and values. If we failed to do our research on candidates and just accepted what they claimed, we should not be surprised when they disappoint us with their votes.

"But," you may say, "Hollywood really creates the culture, doesn't it? They are the biggest influencer in our society." Actually, no. As seen in recent years, Americans have the power to vote with their wallets, and Hollywood cannot function without money. Have you noticed that faith-based films have become more mainstream? The Christian music industry has grown tremendously as well. People of faith have supported faith-based films and entertainment to the point that Hollywood has taken notice and has almost been forced to produce more family-friendly content in recent years. Let's be honest: Nothing speaks to the entertainment industry louder than the sound of money in the bank.

Hollywood Is Not Completely to Blame

Of course, the other side to that proverbial coin is the fact that the pornographic and sex trafficking industries, as well as sexually explicit TV shows and movies, are still being consumed by audiences across America. Why? For the same reason. The market demand for them still exists. Which begs the question: Who is consuming such diabolical content? The answer is twofold. The demand is there because evil exists and men's hearts are wicked, but unfortunately, that does not exclude those who claim to follow the teachings of the Bible. Statistics show that addictions to pornography are a growing problem in the church-going population as well as the non-church going population. In a 2016 survey, the Barna Group found that although well below those who do not profess Christianity, four in ten teen or young adult males in the church are "actively seeking out porn at least once or twice a week."[44]

We cannot blame entertainers, producers, corporations, sports stars, or even our schools for the culture we see today. We only have ourselves to blame, and with even more access to more content anytime, anywhere, the church and our faith leaders must become more proactive and bolder about calling people to repentance.

Our culture begins in our homes, our churches, our schools, and our communities. We are the guardians of our culture, our freedoms, and, most of all, our children. God gave us our children, and we are to be the faithful stewards of their minds and hearts. We are to be their life guides, to teach them the moral and natural laws of God, and to exemplify a life of service to God and others. We are "blessed to be a blessing," and that has been the pervading mindset of the average American citizens up until the past fifty years.

Learning A New Term

In their book, *Battle for the American Mind*, authors Pete Hegseth and David Goodwin give a clear description of what they call the "Western Christian Paideia." The Greek term "paideia" means "the blueprint of thought, affections, and narrative through which every one of us views everything in our world. Paideia is the building block of culture."[45]

If you look at various nations and their cultures throughout history, you will find that their "paideia" included the basic beliefs by which their society was united and ordered. It was how they mentored their children in their traditions and how they viewed the purpose of life. This idea of "paideia" is critical to the continuation of any culture and way of life.

America is unique in the world because our forefathers founded our nation on Judeo-Christian principles. Hegseth and Goodwin write:

The Western Christian Paideia, then, is a particular
type of paideia that was intentionally created for a
self-governing people. The Western Christian Paideia
is a singularity in history. It was created specifically to
sustain republics more than two thousand years ago.
Our founding fathers leaned heavily on the Western
Christian Paideia in their debates as they formed the
American Republic. ... The Greeks realized that ... it
might be possible to cultivate a paideia that supports a
self-governing civilization ... This was a world changing idea: education of the young could create a culture
that pursues higher purpose.[45]

For almost thirteen centuries, the dominant beliefs in the basic
tenets of Christianity permeated the culture of Europe and beyond.
Part of that dominant set of beliefs was the understanding that kings
and rulers were still the servants of God and that God's kingdom
was above all earthly kingdoms and rulers. This was part of the
"paideia" which eventually led to the Reformation and the Great
Awakenings, resulting in millions of people desiring to know more
of God by reading His word in their own language.

When this happened, a new wave of devotion to God and the
dictates of conscience emerged. A new understanding of personal liberty and personal responsibility before God began to spread.
Soon tens of thousands of hard-working people were defying the
combined dictates of governments and their state churches by re-
fusing to follow the man-made rules of imposed religion, in order
to follow their own conscience.

They Were Not Without Fault

Some Christian historians have tried to present a perfect picture
of Colonial America, but don't buy it. There were major problems

throughout the colonies, just as there are today. On the other hand, there have been those who have sought to blame the founders and colonial Americans for every ill and conflict in society today. They have planted many doubts in our minds regarding the faith of our Founding Fathers. Even words and documents on records have been either hidden, twisted, or dismissed as irrelevant.

None of them were without fault. Each was very human and failed in areas of their lives just like everyone of us. But we should not be so blinded by our eagerness to decry their faults that we dismiss their words of warning, wisdom, or insight. The majority of those who formed our Constitution were diligent students of government, economics, world history, and law and could read multiple languages. They were standing up to the greatest military power in the world and risking their lives by doing so. There was much at stake and much to consider by a diverse group of leaders who had never attempted to work in unity while representing thirteen very diverse and independent colonies.

The magnitude of the task they faced is unimaginable, and they were clear in their speeches and writings that they were fervently seeking God's help, guidance, and wisdom. It is recorded over and over again in their own words, and I am so glad that we can still read their words today.

Justice John Jay was an incredible intellect and prolific writer. He joined a large group of abolitionists in New York to establish an anti-slavery society during the American War for Independence. Even in the midst of the war, John Jay, Alexander Hamilton, Benjamin Talmadge, and many others who played a key role in winning America's independence, worked to craft and lobby for legislation to end the practice of slavery. John Jay was a signer of the Declaration of Independence, the First Chief Justice of the Supreme Court, author of five Federalist Papers, and President of the Continental Congress of 1777. He wrote a letter to Representative John Murray on October 12, 1816, and left this piece of timeless wisdom for us to remember: "Providence has given to our people the choice of their rulers and it is the duty as well as the privilege and interest of our Christian Nation to select and prefer Christians for their rulers."[46]

Defining Our Own Culture

You might be thinking that all of the historic quotes are interesting, but the culture has changed, and the government has grown since then. What does this have to do with the question of whether or not Christians should be involved in American politics today? Hasn't it changed too much and gone too far? I'm glad you asked!

American culture is the most unique culture in the world. No other country has been called the "melting pot of the world," and no other country has taken such diversity and created such a strong national unity around shared values and ideals. In order to understand the incredible responsibility and opportunity that is ours as Americans today, it is crucial to understand the origin of our "paideia"—our unique culture and belief system. We have been given so much misinformation about it that it is time we corrected the record for ourselves and for the next generation.

Knowing the factual history of our American culture which led to our unique values system will give us confidence to combat the new so called "woke" culture all around us.

After more than a century of successes and failures in the experiment of self-government, the generation of Americans who formed the Constitution had a lot of examples and templates from which to draw. Because of that, American culture relies on the bedrock principles of representative, limited government, freedom of religion (not FROM religion), freedom of speech, freedom of the press, the right to bear arms, the right to self-defense, freedom from search and seizure, the right to a fair trial of our peers, the assumption of innocence until proven guilty and so much more. These principles were agreed upon after much debate, study, and the example of the colonial legislatures for over a century under British common law.

In the end, they agreed on the core principles that had been key to the success of guiding a free society under natural law. They identified that the source of all liberty is God, not the government. Regardless of how corrupt and dysfunctional our political landscape may look to us now, at its very core still shines the light of eternal truth. That eternal flame still flickers expectantly, waiting for the hands of the faithful in each generation to fan it into a blaze for the next.

The Founders' Greatest Gift

Not only were people of faith an integral part of forming the American governmental structure, but our radically new form of government was built to rely on their continued involvement and the continued leadership of people who held a deep faith in God. **To put it bluntly: the framers of the Constitution were counting on you!** Their confidence in the American people to preserve the gift of self-governance is the greatest gift they could have given us.

Be encouraged that there is a way to renew America, and be advised that the way to renewal begins with you! If you truly value freedom over comfort and principle over power, you are a person who can make a difference by being involved. It will seem easy at first, but the longer you are involved, the more you will realize that standing up to the subtlety and deception of those who seek to gain power for the wrong reasons is not easy at all. Self-governance can be messy, ugly, and downright frustrating. But the beautiful hope that we still have today, even in our declining culture, is that the principles upon which our government is founded are timeless and unchanging. Truth is unchanging. If we use the tools that are still at our disposal and if we arm ourselves with a deeper understanding of our system of checks and balances, we can turn our culture and our nation back to its founding ideals and its reliance on Divine Providence.

Counting the Cost

Once you are engaged, the progress might even seem slow, but stick to it. It was made to be slow on purpose, because decisions made too quickly do not allow for thorough debate and many times lead to government expansion. The debate must be won in the public arena, and that is why you must be prepared with a thorough understanding of our unique American history, culture, and form of government.

I live in a community with one of the largest Amish populations in our state. Many times we have told our Amish friends that if the Amish population in Pennsylvania, Ohio, Indiana, and Iowa would turn out to vote, their sheer numbers could make the difference in a presidential election in battleground states. Then in 2020 I read firsthand accounts from Pennsylvania and Ohio of an unusual phenomenon that was happening. I saw pictures and read stories that Amish buggies were lined up at the polling places on election day. In some areas, the Amish voted in large numbers.

After the election, we heard rumblings that some of them felt that it had been a waste of time to vote since the candidate that they had finally decided to support had not won. Many believed that their vote had not made a difference and said that they had "learned a lesson" and would not be voting again.

Perhaps one thing their voting "English" neighbors should have warned them about was the fact that it takes ongoing involvement on every level to reap the results we need in America today. We cannot renew the faith and culture of this country by electing a certain president or voting one time. It is true that if we elect the right people, they will make the right decisions, but most elected offices have term limits. Once their term is done, we will need to elect someone else who will fill their shoes. And while they are serving in office, it is up to us to hold them accountable.

Change will not happen overnight because, frankly, our decline did not happen overnight. It should be a reminder to all of us that involvement can be painful and even disappointing, but neither is a reason to walk away. Former Ambassador to the United Nations, Adlai Stevenson II shared this definition of patriotic duty to country in his speech to the American Legion Convention in New York in 1952, "Patriotism is not short, frenzied outbursts of emotion, but the tranquil and steady dedication of a lifetime."[47]

What To Expect When Getting Involved

If you run for office or help with a campaign, it will definitely be challenging, difficult, and it might sometimes feel ugly and well-nigh impossible. You or the candidate might face a public smear campaign. You might lose. But as it says in the Bible in John 14:1, KJV *"Let not your hearts be troubled."* Just keep in mind that engagement in the public debate and in the "ugliness" of politics is something that, when done correctly by dedicated people of faith, can result in having the opportunity to be a powerful agent for liberty and light.

A perfect example of sheer determination is none other than Abraham Lincoln. He lost a combined five elections to Congress and the Senate before winning one term in Congress. After losing his next re-election to Congress, he eventually won the presidency. If you think today's campaigns are ugly, take some time to research the awful cartoons and caricatures of campaigns from the 1800s, or read the public squabbles in public papers between John Adams and Thomas Jefferson. American politics was never meant to be pretty, easy, or tidy. Someone once compared it to watching sausage being made in a sausage factory, and there is some truth to that. Campaigns have gotten more and more negative, but we must realize that polling shows that negative ads actually work. It is sad, but true. Bad news travels faster than good. It is human nature, so please go into a campaign with that understanding.

As Americans, we not only complain about the political process being ugly and divisive, but the way Washington operates seems to be divisive as well. Many times that is a legitimate concern. When it comes to the convoluted and contentious process of passing laws, it is good to remind ourselves that it was created to be difficult on purpose.

In his testimony before the Senate Confirmation Committee, Justice Antonin Scalia described the messiness of our unique system this way:

> The real key to the distinctiveness of America is the structure of our government ... There are very few countries in the world that have a bi-cameral legislature ... equally powerful. That's a lot of trouble ... to get the same language through two different bodies elected in a different fashion ... The Europeans don't even try to divide the two political powers - the legislative and the chief executive. In all of the parliamentary countries, the chief executive is a creature of the legislature. There's never any disagreement between them and the Prime Minister as there is sometimes between [Congress] and the President ... When there's a disagreement ... they have a no confidence vote, hold a new election, and they get a new Prime Minister who agrees with the legislature. The Europeans look at [the American] system and they say, "It is gridlock!" ... The framers would say, "Yes! That's exactly the way we set it up! We wanted this to be contradicting power." As Hamilton said in the Federalist, "Yes it seems inconvenient, but inasmuch as the main ill that besets us is an excess of legislation it won't be so bad. This was 1787!"[48]

Scalia went on to urge Americans to appreciate the unique separation of equal powers which creates the so called "gridlock" we observe. He pointed out that sometimes a bill is proposed that is not supported by a minority of the members of Congress, and in an effort to protect the voice of the minority as well as the majority, the framers made it easy to stop the forward progress of the bill with any number of measures given to the minority in the two houses of Congress. The intent of the framers was to create a difficult path for legislation in order to force it through many filters before becoming law, all in hopes that the bills that are eventually passed have been thoroughly vetted and debated by all.

When you do get involved—and I pray that you do—remember to put your reputation in God's hands and leave it there. The Bible says that Christ made himself of low or even no reputation in order to come to earth and die for our sins, and we must do the same when offering ourselves as public servants to our friends and neighbors. When you run for office, give it everything you have and remember that patience and principled persistence will win the day and trust God with it all.

The Leaders We Need

So what does it take to be engaged and involved in the public arena?

It takes people who know the truth about America, who are firmly grounded in their personal beliefs, and who are prepared to address the current state of affairs. It takes people with unwavering courage to clean up corruption in the system. It will take some out-of-the-box thinking. It will take innovative solutions to problems that might be decades old. It will take people who have surrendered their reputations and entrusted them to God's care.

It will take people who are anchored in their faith, guided by their convictions, unwavering in their commitment to service, and principled enough to speak truth to power when necessary. It will take extra effort on the part of every concerned citizen to be diligent in researching candidates. (We will discuss that in detail in a coming chapter).

It will definitely take extra time out of your already busy schedule, and it will stretch you out of our comfort zone. It will mean making difficult decisions in the face of intimidations and threats—sometimes politically and sometimes personally.

And finally, it will mean constant reliance on God's sustaining grace to stand boldly for truth.

CHAPTER SIX

"BE VALIANT FOR TRUTH"

It's surprising how many Americans know almost nothing about their ancestry or family heritage, or even know their own family names any further back than possibly their grandparents. To be honest, I was in that same category for many years. My dad used to tease that he was hesitant to go too far back in our family tree for fear of finding horse thieves hanging from the branches. Yet, I had always wondered about my roots.

Due to the advancements in DNA research and the expansion of popular websites that provide easy access to census records, marriage documents, and other genealogical tools, many Americans have been able to find out more information about their lineage. It's amazing to watch people as they discover the stories of their ancestors. Without exception, they feel more empowered and inspired! Sometimes the stories are tragic and sometimes triumphant, but it seems like the sheer act of learning who your family was and what they did with their lives is something that becomes a source of strength and inspiration to each person who gains an understanding of their roots.

In an episode of TLC's "Who Do You Think You Are" TV show, celebrities who have never researched their family roots are given the opportunity to work with genealogy experts. They visit the places their ancestors lived and sometimes find their homesteads or their graves. Whether they are descended from royalty or rogues, heroes or homesteaders, each one is deeply impacted, and they usually decide to take ownership of the legacy they've been given. In one episode, Valerie Bertinelli was standing on the cobblestone streets where her eight-times great-grandfather once lived. With a lump in her throat and tears in her eyes, she said, "I have a lot to live up to!"[49]

Gaining Perspective

In recent years, America seems to have lost her confidence about her role on the world stage. We have become accustomed to being told who we should be instead of knowing who we have always been. We have inherited a fortune of freedom. Our opportunities are simply unmatched when you consider the history of mankind. With that fortune and opportunity, we have also inherited the heavy price that comes with it. There is an inheritance tax that each generation of Americans must pay at some point.

As I write this book, we are watching turmoil, war, conflict, and confusion increase across the globe. The enemies of freedom are arming themselves and finding ways to create unprecedented alliances, focused on our destruction. We are experiencing internal struggles like never before and facing enemies from without as well. With all of that on the horizon, I still believe that the power to overcome all of these threats is in understanding our unique, national "bloodline" of liberty. As I wrote in an article for the *Washington Times* entitled "America's National Identity Crisis: Solved:"

> Our love of peace and freedom has always been precariously balanced with the necessity of defending our rights to those very values. But in recent years, we've seemed to tire of our job of carrying the mantle of liberty for the world ... It's the high price of

freedom that we've started to question or pass off to others. Perhaps we've begun to question its worth because we've forgotten what the world is like without freedom. We've forgotten that "freedom is a fragile thing." (Ronald Reagan)[50]

Family Legacies

About fifteen years ago, I was at an event in our small community and was approached by a kind, wise-looking, middle-aged woman. She wanted to talk to me about the local chapter of the Daughters of the American Revolution. In our conversation, she shared that the library in the city closest to us had the second largest collection of genealogical books in the country. I had never known much about either side of my family, and I was excited at the possibility of having someone with genealogical experience to guide me through researching my family tree.

A few weeks later, I sat in the Allen County Library in Fort Wayne, Indiana, with the names of about five grandparents and almost twenty different books about my family ancestry in front of me. It was one of the most amazing experiences of my life! Going from knowing almost nothing about my heritage to reading details about their lives, excerpts of their personal letters, and written testimony of their character and faith was such a thrill!

One story made me catch my breath and had an immediate impact on my heart. My eight-times great-grandmother, Sarah Walker, was the mother of at least seven children and a devout Quaker. She and her husband owned a few mills along the Brandywine River near Valley Forge, Pennsylvania. During the War for Independence, her first cousin, General Anthony Wayne (for whom the library I was sitting in had been named), had asked for his troops to be allowed to encamp on the Walkers' property so he could be closer to Valley Forge and General Washington during that terrible winter.

She and her husband welcomed the troops, and she personally ministered to the soldiers, bringing them food and special treats and personally nursing the sick. At one point, General Wayne held a trial in her living room and court martialed several men for desertion. Upon hearing that he had condemned the men to execution, Grandma Sarah (as she came to be known) took General Wayne aside and begged him to spare their lives. He did!

Her story was incredible. Her letters to her daughter Priscilla were full of love and the concerns of a mother's heart. In one book, her husband wrote his personal account of her death and what he recorded stopped me in my tracks.

The family were all gathered around her bed, praying and reading Scripture. Each one said their goodbyes as she began to fade. Then, all of a sudden, she sat up with a sudden burst of strength and said with great conviction, "Be valiant for truth!" Then she looked imploringly at each one of them, slowly laid back down and took her last breath.[51] What incredible last words!

A sweet, simple Quaker woman, with her last breath, had used a word that is usually reserved for the battlefield. Being valiant is usually a word that brings to mind a medieval knight or a famous general commanding his troops in war time. But it was the object of her plea that was remarkable and so poignant to me. Is there a more worthy cause than that of truth? Isn't that the very epitome of what we should stand for and cling to? What better thing to be valiant for than truth?

Correcting the Record

As people of faith, does being valiant for truth exclude the realm of politics? Like the story of the young mother at the beginning of this book, it seems that people of faith in today's America have embraced the lie that their faith should not enter the public arena. We have been told that our spiritual leaders should not speak about politics because of the "separation of church and state." It has become an almost permanent part of our American lexicon, and it has been accepted as fact and even "law" by the last few generations. But where did the lie originate and why was it so easily accepted?

There are many books that have been written in recent years attempting to show how and why this has happened. The purpose of this book is not to give the full history of the church, nor to outline in detail how we arrived at our present dilemma, but I will attempt to present a summary survey of the roots of our current cultural decline.

The roots of the societal problems we face today can be traced back almost to the beginning of the nation, but that fact is just an acknowledgment that there is "nothing new under Heaven." To be blunt, the Godless philosophies that have taken root in our culture, from Deism to critical theory, secular humanism, and cultural Marxism are just further proof that the threat of cultural moral decay is constant when the truth and light of God are replaced with man's pride and rebellion. That is the bottom line.

Psalm 14: 1 NKJV says, *"The fool says in his heart, There is no God. They are corrupt, they do abominable deeds; there is none who does good."*

Isaiah 5:20 KJV says, *"Woe to those who call evil good and good evil, who put darkness for light and light for darkness; who put bitter for sweet and sweet for bitter!"*

Our drift away from God has its roots in some of the Deistic philosophies that became prevalent in the mid-1800s. In the early 1900s, there was a purposeful and targeted effort by humanist and progressive philosophers rooted in Marxist and Freudian theories to spread their teachings across Europe. Their ideas were later developed in the Frankfurt School of Critical Theory in Germany, with the goal of "liberating" the world from the "oppression" and the "patriarchal authoritarianism" of the nuclear family as well as the "repressive effects" of Judeo-Christian values on society. This humanistic school of thought was determined to promulgate their so-called "critical theory" in America—and they did. They wrote books, essays, and articles which were widely circulated, articulating their evolutionary and humanistic view of the world and revealing the pride they took in decrying the weakness of faith in a higher being.

Based firmly in humanistic ideas, they believed that the answer to the oppression of authority can be found in our own minds. Liberated man was "the answer" and would create technology and psychological advancements that would overcome the abhorrent bounds of biology, nature, and any traditional authoritarian structure. Before the outbreak of World War II, several of these critical theory philosophers became professors and teachers at America's most prestigious universities. Their lectures and writings were soon making the rounds with the intellectual elites in a concerted effort to upend traditional values and replace the American culture. They redefined broadly accepted terms to change absolutes and create confusion, all under the guise of man's true "liberation."

In his recent book, *The Rise and Triumph of the Modern Self,* Carl Trueman gives a clear explanation of the origins of the Marxist Left in America and the huge cultural shift we experienced once these critical theories took root. Trueman writes:

> Critical theory may have moved well beyond the writings of ... Herbert Marcuse, Wilhelm Reich, Simone de Beauvoir, and Shulamith Firestone—but the work these earlier thinkers did both established and exemplified the trajectories along which later critical theory has moved ... Reich ... stands in a line of Marxist thinking that sees the family as a problematic bourgeois (ruling) institution. This connection between the family and political oppression is of lasting significance for left-wing politics: the dismantling and abolition of the nuclear family are essential if political liberation is to be achieved.[52]

The Plot of the Critical Theorists

There was a concerted effort on the part of humanistic philosophers to prove the prowess of man's intellect and to remove God from our societal consciousness. Because these intellectual elitists viewed faith as weakness, they started with the evolutionary premise that man is autonomous and self-defining. Faith in science replaced faith in God; never mind that the largest advancements in modern science were achieved by people of faith working within and understanding the bounds of God's natural laws.

Trueman goes on to explain that Rousseau made identity psychological. He then observes that Freud made psychology and identity sexual. When those are combined with Marxist philosophy, the end result is that identity and sex both ultimately become political.

This explains and illuminates why we are facing the seeming insanity we see running rampant in society today. These humanistic philosophies, when combined together, have an end result of transforming society politically by twisting our perceptions of ourselves and our relationship to God. Essentially, these humanists elevate man to the position of God, and as Trueman states, they place "… psychological categories at the heart of revolutionary discourse."[53]

This is why we see lawsuits and lawlessness across America today. Historically, the tangible persecution of a person, such as a physical attack, starvation, or the denial of basic rights of personal safety, personal property, and other measurable, protected rights are the issues given priority. Instead, today, the protection of someone's psychological identity is of the utmost priority because in this humanistic culture, it is critical to elevate man's ability to overcome the physical mistakes of evolution and ultimately society. The question remains: Who determines whether someone's identity and in turn their emotional and psychological well-being have been harmed? They do, or the state decides it.

Is it measurable to determine how much "psychological" damage is done to someone who is offended by your personal religious convictions? It is not. Their offense at your religious viewpoint simply cannot be measured within the bounds of natural law because it does not recognize those bounds. When those boundaries are no longer recognized, society begins to use the currency of offense as its most valuable form of transaction. Soon they reward the loudest victim while punishing those who refuse to be victims, and inevitably, anarchy ensues. The ancient words of Cicero still ring true when he described natural law as true law:

> True law is right reason in agreement with nature; it is of universal application, unchanging and everlasting … It is a sin to try to alter this law, nor is it allowable to repeal any part of it, and it is impossible to abolish entirely.[54]

These critical theory philosophers, following the ideas of Antonio Gramsci and others, put in motion a long-term plan to fundamentally change America by capturing the hearts and minds of our children. Every time socialism and communism fail to achieve utopian goals, these humanist philosophers regroup, reassess, and try again somewhere else on the next unsuspecting population.

Instead of recognizing the absolute failure of their Marxist experimentation, which ended up costing the lives of millions of innocent people under Stalin, Gramsci came up with a new theory. He believed that the cultural humanists could win over the working class by becoming what he called "organic intellectuals." This concept was adopted by the disciples of the Frankfurt School of Critical Thought and efforts were made to implement that approach in America and other nations. Their goal was to create a political revolution by way of infiltrating schools, universities, curriculums, and even the media.[55]

How the Socialist Humanists Philosophy Became Mainstream

With their writings, lectures, and articles, they also planted the seeds for the sexual revolution of the 1960s, and the disciples of this Godless movement continued to infiltrate American culture at every level. It all sounded so good, didn't it? Freedom. Love. Peace. Those behind the critical theory movement wanted to remove the biological limitations of our human bodies and allow the mental and psychological part of man to be unfettered—unlimited in its ability to seek gratification and explore its own desires.

Soon, their students were members of the media, authors, schoolteachers, and politicians who began efforts to rewrite educational curriculums, upend value systems, pass laws restricting religious expression, promote evolutionary theories, and discard the Judeo-Christian virtues upon which America was built.

Existentialist and feminist philosopher Simone de Beauvoir was a critical theory activist in the 1970s, writing several books and articles and speaking extensively on the ultimate goals of the Marxist philosophy. She and others viewed the limitations of biology as almost tyrannical. They viewed the functioning human body as a tyrannical form of authority over what they viewed as their rights of expression. They despised the woman's function in reproduction as a limitation to equality between the sexes. What God created to be beautiful, they viewed as a mistake by evolution—a mistake to be overcome with their intellect and scientific medical advances.

De Beauvior even viewed the female body as a problem—an obstacle to the liberation of pursuing sexual desires without consequence. Therefore, when science invented any kind of birth control, whether it was by pill or via abortion, in the minds of the humanist philosophers, those scientific advancements became the triumph of the human evolutionary journey in finding liberation for women over their physical limitations. It became a "right" to be fiercely protected.[56] This is where the concept of abortion being a basic right has its roots. After all, it finally gave women sexual "equality" with men. Or did it?

What I find both ironic and tragic is that, in their quest for equality, these feminists were essentially desiring to become just like men in every way. As they did so, and supposedly escaped the consequences of promiscuity which came with their newfound liberated sexuality, the emotional, spiritual, physical and psychological repercussions of their own rejection of the laws of nature and God were not avoided—they were compounded. Depression, anxiety, long-term health issues, side effects from birth control measures, and many more problems were experienced by women who embraced the lies of the cultural humanists. Today, there are many support groups for post-abortive women who have had to overcome the tragic effects of abortion. Gender dysphoria has morphed into the transgenderism we see today and is a direct result of cultural humanism's rejection of the natural laws of God.

The Bottom Line

As society takes this rebellion against God, against biology, and against the laws of nature even further, we are now witnessing the horrific rationalization of the mutilation of young children in the transgender movement. The majority of the next generation have accepted the false belief that the human intellect can overcome our physical bodies—that we can correct the mistakes of our own creation (in their minds, evolution) with science and technology. This trend has been growing and only now, after decades of allowing it to creep into our culture, are we seeing the devastating results in the lives of those affected - namely - our children. Pride and rejection of God's natural order has taken us to the same place it always does— dissatisfaction, brokenness, the slaughter of the innocent, and our ultimate ruin.

The Second Goal of Critical Theory: To Rewrite and Undermine American History

As the disciples of humanistic and progressive philosophies began to rewrite American history, they cherry-picked from the writings of the Founders to create a narrative that fit their agenda. For example: the "separation of church and state" idea is a sentence from a letter by Thomas Jefferson which used the phrase in the context of explaining the Bill of Rights. By repetition without context, this "principle" was established as fact in American society. History teachers and educational resources have been teaching that phrase without context in our schools for so long that, over time, the American public now believes it to be part of the Constitution. Politicians, educators, lawyers, and pundits have all repeated the quote for decades, as if it is sacred to our form of government. Thus, the misconception has become accepted as fact.

These critical theorists also chose to discourage people of faith from being involved in the political arena for the purpose of gaining power in the halls of academia and government. They understood the power of the nuclear family and the influence of faith in American culture, so they had to start by removing those two roadblocks in order to achieve the revolution and ultimate liberation of mankind. They knew that those who held traditional views and respected God-ordained authority might be convinced to stay silent if they convinced them that they were following the rule of law. If they could silence the moral majority, then they would be able to usurp the authority of the classroom, the government, the father, the mother, the church, and eventually society as a whole.

We must understand that those who follow the teachings of the critical humanist theories truly believe that their intellectual and psychological prowess gives them a better understanding of what constitutes a free society. They truly believe they are superior and further evolved.

Because their premise is the complete opposite of a faith-based worldview, they see government as the means to control society and guide it to their elitist, utopian ideals. They see schools and educational curriculums as the easiest and most effective means to create disciples who will march in lockstep with their theories and who will become the societal disruptors that they need to overthrow the cultural norms which made America great. Are we not seeing their disciples in action today on college campuses and in violent demonstrations in America?

If any of this is helping you to put the missing pieces of the puzzle in place, then I hope you also understand how much is at stake and how little time we have to do something about it. The terms and definitions of our language are being hijacked and our children are being targeted by those whose end is to redefine freedom to fit their end goal: a humanistic, hedonistic society without God.

Our Responsibility Remains

As ugly and almost abhorrent as the current political climate seems to be, we must take more ownership of our responsibility as Americans. We cannot ignore the fact that engagement in our own governance is not only our birthright, but also our duty as Americans. When neglected, that duty is quickly assumed by those who seek power and control.

It is not enough that we cling to truth if we do not use that truth in action. It is not a choice of faith over politics. The fact is, we will have no freedom to proclaim truth if we do not wield the sword of truth in the political arena while there is still time to do so.

Experts and pollsters estimate that since the 2012 election, more than 40% of evangelical Christians in America did not even take the time to vote, and each election cycle that number is increasing. In a 2009 survey of Generation X Americans, the Barna Group found that only 9% held a biblical worldview and that only

34% (one-third) of Americans believe that moral truth is absolute and unchanged by circumstances.[57]

A report entitled "In U.S., Decline of Christianity Continues at Rapid Pace," the Pew Research Foundation reports:

> In Pew Research Center telephone surveys conducted in 2018 and 2019, 65% of American adults describe themselves as Christians when asked about their religion, **down 12 percentage points over the past decade.** Meanwhile, the religiously unaffiliated share of the population, consisting of people who describe their religious identity as atheist, agnostic or "nothing in particular," now stands at **26%, up from 17% in 2009.**[58] (emphasis added)

Many surveys and polls report that Americans tend to choose their elected representatives based on the stances they take on practical issues like reducing the deficit, providing safe infrastructure, and national defensee—more than basing their voting choices on a candidate's stance on moral issues. However, if someone's morals are questionable, if their worldview is skewed toward humanistic philosophy and self-promotion, then their approach to decision making on every issue should be in doubt as well. Many faith-based efforts like My Faith Votes, Values Voters Summit by Family Research Council, Pro-Life voters guides, and others have been working to address this mindset and help faith-based voters to realize the importance of electing moral leaders.

Worldview Matters

A person's worldview is the filter which assists them in making decisions. It gives them the ability to make sense of vast amounts of information, complex human relationships, individual and collective experiences, and opportunities which life presents. A worldview helps to solidify and give absolutes in what a person believes to be true and ultimately what they value. If they believe in the intrinsic value of life as a gift by God, that will dictate their decision-making regarding animal cruelty, child abuse, abortion, and other choices they face in life.

Those who hold a humanistic worldview will make decisions much differently and have their own set of values. Morals are also dictated by worldview. With flowery words and empty promises that sound so inspiring and even "patriotic," those who see the government as the answer to societal problems say whatever is necessary to win an election, because their worldview allows them to do so.

The sad fact is that we have been watching this trend for quite a while and it is no coincidence that it coincides with the gradual decline of dedicated people of faith serving in the public arena. Of course, we all know that political or governmental involvement is *not* required of anyone in America, but the Founders believed that, when given the chance, the vast majority of citizens would count the opportunity to have a voice in their government as a privilege as well as a means of defense for their liberties.

There is no doubt that the United States of America has been blessed to have been given the greatest form of government the world has ever known. Our nation has enjoyed more freedom and opportunity, more success and progress, more understanding and advancement, more prosperity and peace than any nation in the annals of history.

Our government founded on God's natural law was purchased by the first generation and given as a gift to be safeguarded by each succeeding generation. At times it was safeguarded by a majority and at times by a remnant. I pray that in our generation there will be found at least a remnant of the faithful who will fight boldly to renew our natural rights and to gift them to the next.

When people of faith take up the mantle of responsibility and are "valiant for truth," we will not only renew our nation, but the light of the truth we share will shine brightly to the entire world.

CHAPTER SEVEN

GENERATIONAL LESSONS & COMING THREATS

Have you ever taken a counseling course or attended a counseling seminar? It is a fascinating study in human nature, learned thought processes, and patterns of behavior. It can be quite eye-opening about your own personal failings and ways to guard against areas of weakness you might have. If a person comes from a family where a parent had an addiction or was abusive in some way, a phrase that is often used to describe their success in overcoming those issues is "breaking the generational cycle."

People can get caught in a generational cycle of poverty, abuse, addiction, government reliance, codependence, and many other things. The pattern of parental behavior observed and experienced by the child affects them deeply. If the actions of the parent were positive and encouraging, the child usually emulates that behavior when they become a parent. Of course, no parent is perfect, and for some reason, children tend to absorb whatever weaknesses even good parents have. Those parents who present mainly negative behavioral patterns usually pass those on as well. But every once in a while, a child is able to observe bad behavior and determine that they will not follow in their parents' footsteps. That is the rare exception, but it does happen. The majority of the time, those deeply ingrained behaviors which children learn early on in life are extremely hard to unlearn. It takes time, commitment, and determination to develop new thinking patterns. With the right help and a desire to truly change, it is possible for people to break that generational cycle and avoid the consequences of a negative pattern of behavior.

America has the incredible advantage of good parenting. It wasn't perfect, but it was historically miraculous in many ways. We were given the freedom and the tools not only to live according to our conscience, but also to correct patterns of behavior and adjust our own societal wrongs.

When we close our eyes to the historic failures of other governments and even those of our own, we are in danger of repeating a negative generational cycle. As we have seen from the earliest days of America, we have always been a diverse nation united by shared goals and ideals.

Now, look carefully at our tax system and the categories on our government forms. Look at the woke school curriculums being taught in our schools or how college scholarships are structured. Look at our places of worship and the polarization of political groups. For decades, Americans have been separated and categorized in every conceivable way. The great American patchwork quilt has been unraveling because of the increased polarization of our society, and it did not happen by accident.

Don't Let Our Diversity Divide Us

People's perception of those they disagree with politically has been tainted by an inflammatory and sensational media trying to increase "clicks" with their attention-grabbing headlines and efforts to keep us in our proper "categories." As we look back to gain perspective, we must be willing to face the truth—both good and bad. We must be ready to forgive the wrongs that have divided us and unite for the battles ahead. We are a nation of diverse people from all over the globe, united by the ideas and principles of liberty. We have been brought together, not by blood, but by common goals, beliefs, hopes and dreams. If we focus on what unites us, we can change our course.

Today, those with power and influence are targeting our diversity to make it a weakness and divide our nation by race, political party, faith, and other issues. They have sown seeds of distrust and hate in our society, trying to weaken us from within, and they have been successful in many ways. Unfortunately, it seems like the clock is ticking on our opportunity to renew our nation to its founding ideals. The grip of socialism, humanism, and progressivism is becoming tighter on our nation every day, and we are starting to see more severe repercussions for those who take a stand for their religious freedoms. None of us should imagine that we are exempt, and we should know what is headed our way.

ESG, the UN, and the Threat to America

If you haven't heard of Environmental, Social, Governance (ESG) scores or Social Scores, I implore you to study both. In an article for the American Institute for Economic Research titled, "The Rise of ESG, Replacing Profits with Paternalism, and Strategy with Standards," Kimberlee Josephson explains how the concept of demanding and enforcing politically acceptable behavior has turned into a rising threat to freedom. She states, "Corporate Social Responsibility (CSR) is no longer about giving back or even paying it forward—it is about engagement with social issues—and this is now expected of all firms. The pressure to 'do good' is not only based on reputational concerns from private actors, but derived from a broader, more politically charged global movement."[59]

Do you remember the Green New Deal? That legislation was a direct descendent of the ESG laws passed at the United Nations. It was an effort to enact similar laws in America. After the bill itself failed, bits and pieces of it were used as amendments and passed in other bills in Congress. The pieces that passed have been implemented in a variety of ways, and unless Congress takes swift action to reverse them, you might be experiencing the effects of the regulations in your business and community very soon.

The ESG-based laws gaining ground around the globe come after a long line of UN global agreements, including the 2006 Principles for Responsible Investment and the 2015 Sustainable Development Goals. The global humanistic socialists have been working at this for a long time.

Between 2012 and the present, American companies that do business internationally have been restructuring and preparing to comply with these new ESG directives from the United Nations. Reuters reported in June 2022, "The EU law requires certain large companies to disclose information on the way they operate and manage social and environmental challenges."[60] At first, the response from global business was very positive and they eagerly implemented ways to give back to society or protect the environment, making it a prominent point for best practices. They shared their philanthropic actions in marketing campaigns for their company to attract investors and to hire younger talent. Predictably, the globalists decided that those corporate efforts weren't enough.

The UN Corporate Sustainability Reporting Directive passed in 2022 and establishes strict requirements for big corporations to provide public, digital reports on their efforts and to document their commitment to the pre-approved social causes like improving sustainability for the environment and other green agenda initiatives.

These laws which are being implemented now are in lockstep with social experimentations which took place in the early 2000s in China. In several provinces, Chinese citizens were graded on their participation in state-authorized charities, their support for state-approved policies, and their social behavior. Punishments ranged anywhere from being banned from air travel to having a pet dog taken away. Everyone had access to see your "social score" and the consequences for non-compliance were devastating.

Coming To America

Over the past two decades in America, we have watched kind, Christian people of retirement age who run small businesses like florist's shops, bakeries, daycares, and photography services taken all the way to the Supreme Court for daring to follow the dictates of their own conscience. We have seen businesses audited multiple times by the IRS because of their owners' political leanings. We have seen pastors who merely pray outside abortion clinics suddenly arrested at gunpoint and their homes raided by the FBI in front of their frightened children. We have seen private Christian schools and colleges denied funds from school choice programs because they will not permit co-ed dormitories or recognize multiple genders. Persecution has stepped from our doorstep into our foyer, and we should take note of what else might be coming our way in the near future.

As we shake our heads in disbelief that this could even happen in America, we must realize that it could be a direct result of decades of political silence by people of faith. There truly is a spiritual price to political silence.

I was speaking at a rally for people of faith who had come to learn more about being engaged in the political process and I shared the stage with a pastor from a state on the west coast. The persecution he and his church had endured during the COVID lockdowns was unimaginable. They had shown great character and courage in standing boldly for their freedoms and had paid a great price for it. Huge financial fines, court hearings, media attacks and more had been endured by the people of his church. After the program, I was talking to him in further detail and he told me that he truly believed that the hardships they had experienced at the hands of their state and local government could have been avoided if the church denomination had not discouraged church leaders from speaking out on topics that they considered to be too political. He told me that it had been the policy of the church denomination to be non-political and to admonish the pastors not to get involved in anything that was considered too political. This had been the policy of the denomination for decades. In retrospect, he shared that he believed that they had made a mistake. If they had been more open and given pastors more freedom to encourage civic engagement, they might have had governmental leaders who would have protected their rights instead of threatening and intimidating them.

Let's take that thought a little further to where we stand now, as I write this book. A vast majority of the legacy media and those who adhere to socialist principles on the left have begun to use terms like "Christan Nationalists" when referring to people who they consider to be radical threats to the country. By using this term, they are beginning to set the table for further persecution for people of faith. The term "nationalist" has negative undertones because it harkens back to the Nazi Germany era right before World War II. The strategy is clear. The groundwork is being laid for the general public to view people of faith it's close-minded, radical and a threat to the government.

Case in point: During the COVID lockdowns, schools were shut down and parents began to hear the lessons being taught to their children. Parents became more aware of the extreme ideologies being used to indoctrinate their children and they began to organize into groups who wanted to address the issues. In Virginia, there was a large movement of parents upset about critical race theory, DEI programs, transgender attacks on young girls in restrooms, and much more. After hundreds of parents attended school board meetings, expressing their concerns in respectful and reasoned pleas using the proper channels, it was discovered that the FBI and other government agencies were adding the names of law-abiding parents to their terrorist watch lists because they considered those parents to be a threat to the government.

It is my contention that this is only the beginning. The strategic changing of specific definitions for words and phrases that we thought we understood is a way to upend our culture and create division in our society. Freedom is defined differently when you believe that freedom is granted by the government instead of by God. Patriotism is viewed by many in the younger generation to be just as negative as nationalism in Nazi Germany because this new generation has been taught that our nation is rooted in prejudice, racism, and radical religious beliefs. Religion is seen as a crutch used by the weak or unscientific.

If people of faith do not stand up and get involved at all levels of government, we will be paying the price of our silence. We have a moral and spiritual obligation as people of faith in America to break out of our silence and speak boldly for truth in the public arena. If we wish to continue being the salt and light that we have been for centuries, we must be salt and light in our own government as well.

Warnings from China

The latest news coming out of socialist or communist countries should serve as a dire warning. Just the other day, I received an update from an organization called Voice of the Martyrs. They help Christians all over the world who are under persecution. The email stated that in July of 2018, a Christian Chinese pastor named Pan Yongguang was visiting with a fellow pastor in Chengdu. Over lunch, his friend Wang Yi asked Pastor Yangguang a poignant question. He asked, "Are you prepared to be arrested?" With the realization that the Chinese communist party was increasing its control over churches and restricting the lives of Chinese Christians, Pastor Yongguang gathered his church to discuss their options. Sadly, five years later in 2023, Pastor Wang Yi is serving a nine-year sentence in prison in the Jintang Prison, located in the Sichuan province. The email reports:

With more persecution on the horizon and concerns about their ability to raise and instruct their children in biblical truth, the congregation made a difficult and drastic decision: They would leave China. Tune in ... to hear an update on the "Mayflower Church" from Pastor Pan. Learn how they are .... studying English and hoping ultimately to resettle in the U.S.[61]

They are hoping, planning, and praying to be able to come to America. This "Mayflower Church" is an echo of the Separatist Pilgrims from the church at Scrooby Manor in England who landed at Plymouth in 1620. I wonder how they will find us if they are ever able to arrive? Will they find us to be on the same road toward the religious persecution they fought so hard to escape? It is sad to think that they might find similar oppression in the new 'woke" America once they arrive.

A North Korean Refugee Calls Out Woke Culture

Another example of our rapid decline was described by a recent North Korean immigrant, Yeonmi Park. She narrowly and miraculously escaped North Korea with her mother when she was just a young girl. Once they arrived in a rural town in China, her mother was brutally raped and sold into sex trafficking, and so was Yeonmi. Somehow, after crossing the Gobi Desert and enduring unimaginable trauma, she found her way to America. She is a brilliant young woman and was eventually accepted to Columbia University. Since 2015, she has publicly excoriated the university and other elite institutions for their "woke" agenda and for teaching similar indoctrination to what she experienced under a brutal communist dictatorship. As the *New York Post* reported, Park said: "I realized, wow, this is insane. I thought America was different, but I saw so many similarities to what I saw in North Korea that I started worrying."

She told the *Post* that she was shocked at the amount of "self-censoring" she was asked or even required to do by one of America's top Ivy League universities. She said, "I literally crossed the Gobi Desert to be free and I realized I'm not free, America's not free ... Every problem, they explained to us, is because of white men."[62]

She went on to explain that some of the instructions she received regarding white privilege were not very similar to the caste system she had experienced in communist North Korea. She pointed to the fact that people in North Korea were categorized based on their lineage and ancestry. One of the saddest statements I have read in recent years was when she said, "I thought North Koreans were the only people who hated Americans, but it turns out there are a lot of people hating this country in this country."

In her 2014 memoir called *In Order to Live*, Park shares her harrowing experiences under the brutal Communist regime, her perilous escape from her native country, and her survival of being trafficked in China. Her shock at how "willingly" Americans are giving their rights away is well founded. As she describes it, "Voluntarily, these people are censoring each other, silencing each other, no force behind it. Other times (in history) there's a military coup d'etat, like a force comes in taking your rights away and silencing you. But this country is choosing to be silenced, choosing to give their rights away."[63]

Have we been too silent in the face of threats to our freedoms? Have we allowed ourselves to be intimidated by the "woke warriors" in our schools and in the media who are spewing hatred and disdain for our history, morals, and beliefs? Our founders, human as they were, actually upended historically accepted norms by allowing those with deeply held religious beliefs to play an active role and to have ongoing influence in government. This was almost radical at the time. It is still radical when you compare the freedoms we enjoy today to those of the rest of the world. We should never allow ourselves to be shamed, intimidated, or silenced because of our religious beliefs, the color of our skin, or our political principles. Never!

Lessons from Tiananmen Square

Do you remember the young man who stood in front of a military tank in the middle of Tiananmen Square in Beijing, China, in 1989? He was part of a grassroots, organic protest after the death of Hu Yaobung, General Secretary to the Chinese Communist Party. Yaobung had advocated for democratic reforms after the brutal reign of Mao Zedong had ended. College students started gathering publicly to mourn his death, but the public gatherings in cities across China continued longer than anyone expected. Soon, in memory of Yaobung and inspired by the pro-democratic lectures of astrophysics professor Fang Lizhi, the demonstrators began to formulate a list of reforms that they wanted to see enacted.

After some selective reforms in the early 1980s which had attempted to address the structure of the economic markets, the country had fallen into turmoil. The elites had been given advantages and the disparity between the upper class and lower class had grown worse. The one-party political system had lost credibility, and the list of grievances by the young demonstrators included the following: skyrocketing inflation, government corruption, restrictions on political involvement, freedom of the press, and freedom of speech. Do any of those issues sound familiar?

Thousands took to the streets and marched in the square. This lasted for over two months, until the leaders of the CCP declared martial law and gave orders to attack their own people—unarmed, peaceful demonstrators who had tried to make their case with hunger strikes, lectures, and signs. Hundreds and possibly thousands were slaughtered. Hundreds were taken into custody and put in jail without any court hearing, bail, or recourse. An image of one college-aged young man facing down an oncoming Chinese military tank alone in Tiananmen Square sent shockwaves around the world. He was willing to face a tank in order to gain just a small taste of freedom.

Since then, the Chinese government has renamed the Tiananmen Square massacre and referred to it with a variety of "politically correct" names—a riot, an incident, an event, and most commonly its date, June 4th. We don't know what happened to the thousands who were arrested in the demonstrations, and perhaps we never will.

This and many other stories throughout history should be a lesson to us in what happens when a government becomes tyrannical, godless, and corrupt. When the "elected" officials are actually chosen or bought by the government and become pawns of the state instead of representatives of the people, very soon we will be so desperate for a little taste of freedom that we could be the next young man standing alone in the public square looking down the barrel of a military tank.

Facing Our Present Reality

When we acknowledge the road down which we are heading, and when we understand what is at stake, I pray that our apathy regarding the immense privilege we have to take part in civic engagement is finally corrected. Engagement in our governmental system is our birthright.

If you are one of the millions of Americans who are shocked at the increasing attacks on our religious freedoms, you are not alone. It is truly shocking to see how fast our freedoms are being threatened and taken away. Many times government overreach is excused because of someone's bad behavior. Those proposing the restrictions of our natural rights claim that the existing law wasn't strong enough or it was too harsh. The arguments can be heard on every news channel and read on every social media platform.

We would be wise to look past the haze of misinformation to the root of the problem. Sometimes, a societal problem cannot be solved by passing more laws or repealing others. The root of envy, hatred, prejudice, selfishness, pride, or greed is found in the heart. When we reach hearts by being salt and light and by electing those who will stand for truth, we will change the moral compass of the nation; but if we retreat from the public square and allow people to gain power who would demand that we exchange our freedom for an empty promise of security, then we deserve neither freedom nor security. Perhaps William Shakespeare put it best in his classic play, *Macbeth*, when the character of Hecate says, "And you all know that security is mortals' chiefest enemy."[64]

In order to keep America free for those who continue to seek refuge here and in order to continue the good work of God both at home and around the world, we must be knowledgeable about our history, informed on current events, and prepared to help elect those who are committed to protecting our natural rights. When we do this, we will be providing the legacy of a positive generational cycle for the next generation.

CHAPTER EIGHT

THE GLOBAL INFLUENCE OF THE AMERICAN CHURCH

"Let not anyone pacify his conscience by the delusion
that he can do no harm if he takes no part and forms
no opinion. Bad men need nothing more to compass
their ends than that good men should look on
and do nothing."

-JOHN STUART MILL, 1867 INAUGURAL ADDRESS, UNIVERSITY OF ST. ANDREWS[65]

It can be discouraging when you look at the present landscape of our nation. As I write, inflation is on the rise and there is a growing disparity between those who have power and access to economic advantages and those who do not. For decades, our freedom of speech has been under attack in many ways, but we have won many battles to preserve it as well. There is corruption in our government and immorality in our culture. Our children are being targeted and our foundations seem to be crumbling. Although it seems that hope is almost lost, it is still *our country and it is still the* government of "we the people." It is still a constitutional democracy within a republic and we are still allowed to take part.

The easy route would be to wash our hands of the moral decay, bury our heads in the sand, and try to stay out of it. But the easy route will not solve our problems.

We cannot limit our lives to a small circle of work, church, school, and family and expect the country to stay on the right path. How can we fill our lives with seemingly good things while ignoring our responsibility as citizens and then whine and complain about how morally bankrupt our country has become? America does not have an autopilot function. We are responsible for the state of our culture, and what we do echoes around the world.

The Exportation of American Immorality

A few years ago, on a Congressional delegation trip to countries which had been part of the former Soviet Union, my husband and I had the amazing opportunity to meet with a variety of elected officials in the various nations we visited. One evening, we were at a reception and were engaged in conversation with a middle-aged man who was very excited to talk to us about possible trade with America. He eagerly shared with us the amazing agricultural and manufacturing products they produced there and wanted to know our perspective on opening up different avenues of trade. His was a country which adhered to a very traditional and orthodox form of Christianity, and so they encouraged young married couples to have large families and to be faithful to raise their families in the church.

He eagerly shared with us that his country loved our dedication to freedom and elected representation, but then he paused and said, "We do love a lot of things that you export, except your morals. I hope you don't mind my bluntness, but the American morals that come to us via American movies and music are corrupting our young people. We could do without that."

He laughed nervously, hoping he had not offended us, but we knew exactly what he meant. We were speechless for a moment because he was right. All we could do was agree and let him know that we didn't blame him for speaking the truth. That conversation happened several years ago, and unfortunately, things have not gotten any better since then. Now we face dire consequences and the looming threat that immorality and corruption will soon bring our nation to ruin. That is the challenge of our generation.

What has happened to the strong influence of the American church in our culture? When did we begin our rapid moral decline? Was it when we allowed our history books to be rewritten? Was it after the Scopes trial when Darwinian evolution was introduced into our educational system? Was it when we removed prayer and Bible reading from our schools?

That question is answered masterfully in several recently published books. As referenced earlier, *The Rise and Triumph of the Modern Self* by Carl Trueman goes into great detail regarding the roots of our cultural decline. He outlines the shift in our focus from a God-centered view of a divinely ordered world, including our understanding of how we fit into that order as individuals, to a self-centered view of the world, focused on the right to self-discovery and the pursuit of personal desires, free from traditional limitations or authority.

Trueman references the theories and writings of Philip Rieff, Charles Taylor, Alasdair MacIntyre, Wilhelm Reich, Herbert Marcuse, and other philosophers who preceded them, like Max Horkheimer and Eric Fromm, the founder of socialist humanism. Trueman writes:

> The modern self and the culture of the modern self clearly find their immediate roots in the intellectual developments that took place in the eighteenth and nineteenth centuries. The most obvious aspect of this influence is the inward, psychological turn with regard to the nature

of self ... It is also clear that the whole notion of sacred order, so critical ... for the preservation and transmission of culture, also begins to collapse. The seeds of today's moral anarchy, where personal emotional preferences are constantly confused with moral absolutes, is thus to be found in the nineteenth century.[66]

Another book which thoroughly outlines the fast decline of the influence of faith in America, approaching the subject from an educational point of view, is the book I have previously referenced, *Battle for the American Mind* by Pete Hegseth and David Goodwin. The authors describe the unique American Western Christian paideia, as including the following fundamental beliefs:

1. There is a creator God
2. Man was created by God in the image of God
3. Natural law exists regardless of man's invented laws
4. Man's laws should honor the natural laws of God
5. Man fell into sin
6. Mankind can be redeemed by God.

These foundational beliefs are key to the Western Christian culture. They were woven into the fabric of our society, and the American government is reliant on their continued existence.

These beliefs are what united us in the principles of freedom, personal discipline, shared values, and self-governance. It created order, stability, and unlimited opportunity for all. They are what sets us apart and what created the abundant success we have enjoyed for centuries.

At a certain point in our history, there was a sudden turning away from the established and successful American culture. As Hegseth and Goodwin explain:

For the first time in two thousand years of cultural history... Progressives had a new understanding of humanity: we are simply the pinnacle of naturalistic evolution. We neither partake in a divine nature, nor have we fallen, because there is no God ... Our Progressive school system ... has ensconced a new worldview based on a new world order ... where history is rejected, science is God, and the state is the temple in which citizen workers worship.[67]

The Church Divided

When the sexual revolution of the 1960s began, conservatives took action against the Marxist, atheistic philosophies which became more visible and began to run rampant in society. During that time period, many Christian schools were founded, evangelistic efforts were intensely undertaken, traditional educational curricula were published, and scientists who believed in intelligent design began to speak out. Sadly, by that time, the progressives were already firmly in control of the public schools and the vast majority of American universities. An entire generation had been raised with progressive ideals and the results, as we have witnessed, were catastrophic.

Interestingly, as I have researched American history, I have discovered that the mainline Protestant churches in America experienced a large divide around the same time that these humanist philosophies were becoming more prevalent. Before the divide in the church, the majority of churches held fast to the longstanding belief that personal faith, guided by the Bible and a tender conscience toward God, should dictate every aspect of life. The majority held to the principle that faith in God's word determines how society as a whole views its own existence and purpose. Until the early 1900s, it was commonly accepted that finding one's divine purpose in life was an achievable goal and that it informed all participation in society, including personal convictions, vocation, church attendance, charity work, public service, education, and child-rearing.

This basic, foundational belief was the fertile soil which produced the fruit of a strong and stable American culture for more than a century. This included service to others, civic engagement, reaching for excellence, new inventions, scientific advancement, and mission work around the world. It created the ability to reason freely within God's ordered world, within His structured laws of nature and the God-ordained institutions of the family, the church, and the government. It gave people the freedom to elevate their thoughts to higher purposes, and it resulted in the greatest scientific and innovative advancements the world has ever seen. Those advancements improved the standard of living for the majority of the world and still affect us today.

Then the church became divided between the traditionalists who held to the fundamental doctrines and the progressives who leaned away from the traditional teachings. The great revivals were led by the traditional side of the church and its leaders. The great movements of the late 1850s led to the far-reaching, evangelistic ministries of D.L. Moody, Sam Jones, Billy Sunday, and many others in the 1870s and 1880s. The latter revivals were focused on spiritual renewal and resulted in a return to faith for tens of thousands around the world. Leading into the 20th century, these evangelical leaders were champions for a return to Biblical principles. While their focus was on evangelism and discipling, the progressive takeover of the American education system continued, undetected and unhindered for the most part.

The Progressive Church

On the progressive side of the church divide were the proponents of the "Social Gospel," a new teaching which attempted to mix the humanistic and evolutionary theories being taught in the schools with the teachings of the Bible. The new progressive

Christians did not accept the Scriptures as inerrant, and because of their acceptance of some of the humanistic philosophies, they began to view the government as the answer to the majority of societal problems instead of seeing the church and the family as the answer. Soon, the proponents of progressivism and the Social Gospel were turning over their normal church responsibilities to the government; responsibilities such as the care of the poor and the widows, protecting women and workers, sobriety, sexual promiscuity, and other social issues.

If you aren't familiar with the term Social Gospel, then you might have heard the term "social justice." It has been a term and a teaching that has been around for many years in the church and has been reinvented many times over.

The Catholic Church and other denominations have used the term in a variety of ways over the years, and in the beginning as well as on its face it sounded like a good thing. Justice is good. Reaching society is good. Addressing injustices in society is good. But just as with the hijacking of other terms in our society, the meaning of the words themselves and the actions that have resulted from the movement have not created the results we would expect. Today, the original movement for social justice has been largely hijacked to promote an agenda being pushed by far-left political activists. The well-meaning origins have morphed into many iterations and the new "woke" culture is only the latest result of that hijacking.

The new goals of those who are warriors for social justice are not to help those who have been left behind, forgotten, or mistreated by society. Instead of ministering to those in need or who have been marginalized in society, the new goals of the movement, include seeking revenge for past wrongs, creating a permanent victim mentality, and spreading the idea that the government is the source of liberty.

Where is revenge found in the scripture? Doesn't the Bible teach us that we are conquerors and victors, empowered by God and His forgiveness and mercy? These teachings being espoused by groups promoting something that sounds so good are the complete opposite of those found in the Scriptures.

Our founding documents lay out a very clear case that our rights and freedoms come from God, not man. The terms "natural rights" and "unalienable rights" are used throughout our founding documents and clearly state that we have always viewed our liberties as being given to us directly by our Creator. To remove that belief and replace it with the belief that the government is the source of our liberties is to empower our government not only with the power to limit our freedoms, but also to remove our freedoms whenever they see fit. This is extremely dangerous!

Devotion to God vs. Scientific Education

A few years ago, I had the privilege to accompany my husband on a diplomatic mission to visit several countries in eastern Europe which had been part of the former USSR. It was a complete education in itself and made us value our beloved nation all the more! At one point we attended a luncheon and were seated with a very kind man from Lithuania. It was a fascinating conversation! I was so curious about his experiences because he had lived under communism, had seen its fall, and was now living in a country with a representative form of government. He hadn't said much during the roundtable discussion before the lunch, so I was eager to know more about his story. I asked him what it was like living under a communist regime. I was surprised at his matter-of-fact reply.

"It was different," he said. "We didn't have much freedom. We couldn't speak or express our opinions much."

"I can't imagine." I commented.

"Yes, it was pretty bad, but you know, it wasn't terrible."

Now I was even more curious. The stories I had been told growing up about the conditions for people of faith under communist regimes had sounded terrible to me. The testimonies of persecution from missionaries who had ministered to those countries were frightening.

"Did you have any level of freedom of religion?" I asked. "I mean, were you able to attend any church of your choosing?"

He smiled kindly and replied, "Of course! We had that. We could go wherever we wanted, as long as we didn't plan to go to college."

I was taken by surprise. I wasn't quite sure what he meant and asked him to explain a little more.

"Well, I mean that we could attend any church we liked. Of course. We had that freedom. But the police kept track of the names."

"The names?" I asked, still not sure that I was comprehending what he was saying. "What names?"

"The names of those who attended the church for services," he replied nonchalantly. "You see, we had complete freedom—you know—freedom of worship as you say—but those of faith were considered lacking in scientific understanding, so they would not be good candidates for higher education."

I was speechless, searching his face for more information. "So, did you go to church?"

"Well." He smiled. "My parents wanted their children to attend university, so we did not go to church. Mind you, it was our choice. So, like I said, we still had freedom, you see? We all had freedom of religion."

Stunned and trying to process what he had just said, I tried to smile and continue the conversation, but my mind was racing. I was talking, but my mind could not let go of the shock of what he had just shared. He had said it so simply and in such a casual, conversational way, that it took me a while to realize the full impact of it all.

Under communism and Soviet rule, people of faith were seen as "simple-minded" and even unintelligent! The fact that they had faith in God was the proof that the government used to decide that they simply were not "scientifically" minded, and therefore they did not meet the government-approved criteria. Therefore they were not qualified to even be considered for higher education. The system gave the people an illusion of "freedom of religion" while forcing them to decide between their faith and the chance for higher education. The government automatically disqualified those who were "too religious" from pursuing higher learning in a variety of fields and limited them to the lower paying jobs of society and, thus, a limited future.

The Effects of Communism on People of Faith

In a 2014 study, the Pew Research Center reported, "During the Soviet period ... people who publicly professed religious beliefs were denied prestigious jobs and admission to universities."[68]

Is America headed in the same direction? Are there certain basic "politically correct" tenets that must be accepted and agreed to in order to receive advancements in certain vocations and sectors of our society? For example, are scientists who believe in creation and intelligent design regularly invited to speak as experts in news reports? Are they given the same respect as those who adhere to evolutionary theories in public debates or school textbooks? When they make new discoveries, are they even cited as Creationists? Are college professors creating an economy of free thought in their university classrooms? As a college student, if you do not agree with the superiority of progressive and critical philosophy or with the "fact" of climate change, are you encouraged to speak about the facts that you believe in, or are you ridiculed? Is your freedom of speech denied? Is your paper or test marked down because you express a Christian or conservative point of view?

Are history teachers who teach the truth about the faith of the Pilgrims asked to give interviews to the media or in documentaries for public television? Who is given preference, and why? If we are honest with ourselves, we must realize that we are actually not that far removed from the old Soviet mentality in America today. We must recognize that in our current American culture, there is a government-approved list of criteria for being accepted as intelligent in educated American society.

More and more, there are politically correct beliefs and requirements imposed on us in order to be considered "informed enough" to participate in politics, education, healthcare, and scientific debates in any public forum. Social media platforms will "hide" a post that doesn't meet the "standards" and your account will be suspended or even shut down if you have too many "conservative" infractions.

Even now, with the implementation of ESG standards, first proposed at the UN and spread across Europe, it won't take much for us to inch closer to the communistic policy of imposing social standards as requirements for educational opportunities. They are already a prerequisite to conduct business around the globe.

The Rise of the American Thought Police

Now, we don't have the military or the police keeping lists of those who attend church, but we do have "thought police" limiting public discourse. It happens in the workplace, on college campuses, and in political dialogues. Conservative lecturers are met with violent demonstrators on college campuses. Our young people have been so indoctrinated against free thought and open dialogue that they are militant in their opposition to even having an honest debate. Facts are denied. History is erased. Religiously based books are being removed or banned by state legislatures. Even Hollywood celebrities and wealthy executives are being canceled by the left who will stop at nothing to destroy the lives of anyone who dares to challenge their worldview.

My sons are now college age, and as I receive emails from various colleges wanting them to consider attending, I have noticed that many are touting their "green campuses" and "sustainability" bona fides. One email encouraged students to consider potential schools based on the school's stand on "sustainability" and whether they have a commitment to a "greener world" because, according to this school, that determines whether the school is serious about protecting future generations. They usually go on to brag about how they have an extensive electric vehicle initiative, how many charging stations they have, or how they have won awards on Climate Leadership or other sustainability standards. The colleges use all of the usual Green New Deal talking points and that makes me wonder how much money they received from the government as incentive for pushing that particular agenda. I also noticed that they mentioned nothing about their efforts to stop the terrible human toll that electric vehicles have taken on poverty-stricken populations in Africa due to mining for cobalt in atrocious, inhumane conditions.

Our family is a farming family and we have always recycled, kept great care of our land, and made sure to be good stewards of the earth that God gave us, but we believe that God values human life over anything else. There is a way to both encourage the study of new technology and innovations in an effort to be even better stewards of the planet God created while also putting a value on every human life around the globe.

The Humanists War on the Family and God's Created Design

In trying to erase God from our society those who adhere to the humanist, progressive view end up replacing God with government. They would never say this in so many words, but in actions, that is exactly what they do. That is one of the reasons they promote the idea that people of faith should not be involved in government.

In their view, the church and faith are not viable answers to their problems because they are not answers that come from the government or the intellect of man. To the humanist progressive, the government becomes the only place which can offer scientifically sanctioned, man-centered solutions.

In their view, the government even determines what is science and what is not. According to the humanists, the nuclear family is public enemy number one! As humanist Marxist philosopher Wilhelm Reich describes in his 1933 book, *The Mass Psychology of Fascism*, "The family is the authoritarian oppressive culture in miniature."[69]

As we move closer to this man-centered, socialist society, with a large swath of society rejecting Judeo-Christian values, we begin to see how society functions without a natural order. Anarchy of the individual mind and society as a whole becomes the norm, and we experience the rise of violent riots in our streets, lack of concern for others, and little to no discipline in our schools. We witness the establishment of a permanent welfare state, growing fatherlessness, the normalization of promiscuity in our youth, a rapid increase in teen suicides, rampant drug addictions, and much more.

The Latest Terms You Should Know

If you haven't heard of Critical Race Theory, Social Emotional Learning (SEL), or the implementation of Diversity, Equity & Inclusion (DEI) officers, please sit down at a computer and do an internet search to find out exactly what these dangerous programs and curriculums are teaching the next generation.

America is usually about twenty years behind Europe in its cultural trends, but we would be wise to take notes from their mistakes and experiences. Young children there who have been treated with experimental drugs, medical treatments, and surgeries, with promises of changing their gender, are now beginning to realize that many of these doctor-prescribed "scientifically advanced" treatments are irreversible. Multiple lawsuits are being filed and lives are being forever altered due to these treatments.

Many have fought to pass new laws to protect children, but for many of these children and families, it is too late. When will the world learn that no matter how many times socialism, communism, or humanism has been tried, it has failed and left a terrible path of human destruction in its wake.

There is a spiritual price to our political silence, but there is still time to speak and the American church still has a chance at global influence.

We can speak truth from our pulpits and to our children and grandchildren. We can write it in books, articles, blogs, and other media outlets. We can monitor our children's school books and be ready with an answer if they are inaccurate or misleading. We can attend school board meetings and town hall gatherings ready to ask informed questions on issues that concern our children and our communities. We can share the truth kindly with teachers and administrators, neighbors, elected officials, prayer group friends, and coworkers.

It's time to step into the public arena armed with the facts and share them confidently by every means necessary. If we believe that our children and grandchildren deserve the same chance at freedom, we must make the necessary sacrifices to ensure they have it. We must take action—*now*!

But where do you even start? It's simple ... and that's next!

CHAPTER NINE

CIVIC ENGAGEMENT - IT'S EASIER THAN YOU THINK

In a democracy, the people meet and exercise the government in person; in a republic, they assemble and administer it by their representatives and agents … Had no important step been taken by the leaders of the Revolution … no government established of which an exact model did not present itself, the people of the United States might … at best have been laboring under the weight of some of those forms which have crushed the liberties of the rest of mankind. Happily for America, happily, we trust, for the whole human race, they pursued a new and more noble course. They accomplished a revolution which has no parallel in the annals of human society. They reared the fabrics of governments which have no model on the face of the globe. They formed the design of a great Confederacy, which it is incumbent on their successors to improve and perpetuate.

- JAMES MADISON, FEDERALIST PAPER #14[70]

It's true confession time, so here goes. I was a fine arts major in college. Yes, I was one of "those." Every chance I got, I auditioned for plays, musicals, and operas and I landed many lead roles. My days were filled with classes, homework, and production rehearsals late into the night. Singing, acting, writing, and performing were all a major part of my college experience. It was inspirational and crazy and challenging all at the same time, and I loved it. After college I became a fine arts teacher, specializing in music, drama, English, and speech in junior high and high school. I enjoyed coaching some girls' sports, and I have to admit that being the junior high homeroom teacher was a blast!

But civics? Most of my education in civics came from my father, who was an avid historian and followed politics with a passion. The rest came from a few US History and Government classes I took in high school. I enjoyed those classes because I truly loved studying history, but I probably didn't retain as much on the civics side as I should have.

Just like so many American families, I remember visiting historic places like Colonial Williamsburg, Plymouth, Massachusetts, and the Gettysburg battlefield with my family when I was in elementary school. We never visited our state house, and I never toured the US Capitol until after I was married. I didn't know what C-SPAN was, and I was never part of a debate team. I never participated in a mock legislative process or had someone teach me Robert's Rules of Order. Only one governor left a definite impression on me as a young person, and that is because he happened to speak at an event where my high school choir was singing. The other reason I remember him was the fact that he was still governor when I got my driver's permit, and I thought it was so neat that it had his signature on it.

I was blessed with a father who followed national issues carefully and who was always teaching us about America's Christian history. He listened to political pundits and news reports and shared a lot with us as we grew up. In 1978, he was invited to attend an intense training seminar on the true story of the Pilgrims, in which he was provided original documents to study.

He made sure that our entire family knew the Pilgrim story in detail, from Scrooby Manor to Leyden, Holland, to Plymouth and everything that happened in between. He also taught us historic facts about George Washington's life story, the writings of John and Abigail Adams, and the intellectual prowess of Thomas Jefferson and John Quincy Adams. I learned from him to study history with a passion, and it was in history books that I discovered the influence that George Mason had on Virginia's many founders of American liberty.

My father also taught me about the genius and generosity of James and Dolly Madison, the determination and wit of Abraham Lincoln, the incomparable intellect and oratory of Frederick Douglas, the unshakable resolve of Susan B. Anthony, the eloquence of Edward Everett Hale, the inspiring story of Francis Scott Key, and the tenacity and audaciousness of Andrew Jackson. We discussed and debated freely about the issues that brought on the American Civil War, and we thrilled over the scientific advancements and genius of George Washington Carver. We thanked God for the faith and leadership of Dwight D. Eisenhower and the vision and courageous leadership of Martin Luther King Jr. We discussed the American death toll of the Roe vs. Wade decision, and so much more. Millions of Americans probably learned those same things growing up as well.

Although I was young at the time, I clearly remember watching Ronald Reagan's many speeches and debates, and although we were never involved in his campaign, we still considered ourselves a part of the Reagan Revolution. I remember the feelings of fear and grief on the day Reagan was shot and I remember gathering around a little black and white TV to watch the Challenger space shuttle launch, and then the horror we felt as we watched it explode in the sky.

Like so many other Americans, my extended family was divided somewhat between the two parties. I had one grandmother who said she had voted Democrat "ever since FDR," and one grandmother who was proudly Republican and worked the polls faithfully every election. They both loved God, loved America, and encouraged their grandchildren to do the same. So, in spite of my passion and focus on fine arts, like so many other Gen X children, I was taught American history and even some current events, faithfully, by my parents, grandparents, and teachers as I was growing up.

At the age of eighteen, with all that knowledge about American history and current events, I was still nowhere near as prepared as I should have been when they handed me my first ballot. What was a State Representative again? What did Commissioners even do? We had a Town Council? I had to choose three of the ten names? I remember reading all of the names, trying to remember seeing any yard signs or commercials that might help me decide.

Where To Start

Does any of this sound familiar? I share all of this to say that being engaged in the political process is possible for any American, regardless of your upbringing, college major, vocation, experiences, or training. I'm living proof of that!

In this chapter, I want to share some very practical ways that you can get involved and make a difference. Consider it your how-to guide for civic engagement. Now, more than any time in history, it is amazing how much access we have to information! Once we discuss the incredible resources we have at our fingertips, we will go through the wide variety of ways that you can be involved and make a difference. Once you have solid resources for reliable information, I encourage you to do even further study on your own.

I want to ask you a series of questions, and I want you to try to answer them honestly. This exercise is a good way to assess how involved and informed you have been in the American political system and to figure out the underlying viewpoint that you were surrounded by as you grew up as an American. Ask yourself the following questions:

1. How many names or faces of your elected officials (state and federal) did you know or even recognize growing up? Do you remember hearing their names at all?
2. How many members of your church ever attempted to run for office at any level?
3. Have you known the names of your state senators, city councilmen, or your US Congressman at any time in your life?
4. Did you ever meet any of the above-mentioned office holders or see them in person?
5. Did you ever participate in a political campaign or attend an event supporting them?
6. Can you name your US Senator today? AND do you know how long they have held the office?
7. Do you know the difference between a State Representative and a Congressman?
8. Do you know when your county political central committee meetings are held?
9. Have you ever attended a Commissioners meeting, a city or county council meeting, or a school board meeting?
10. Do you know how to find out when local officials are holding receptions, fundraisers, or roundtable discussions in your community?

If your answer is yes to any or all of those questions, then congratulations! You are the rare exception. If not, I hope that this book will be an encouragement to you with how simple it is to become more involved in your government and have a voice in your community.

Even if they have not been involved in the election side of American government, the great majority of American people of faith DO have a close tie with someone who served in the armed forces. That specific aspect of involvement in public service and duty to our country has not faltered, at least not yet. Perhaps because of the negative stigma associated with politics, we have opted to offer our contributions more in the form of serving to defend and protect our nation. It is the more noble and sacrificial form of service, and the numbers are clear that we have had a great percentage of participation in that noble calling. Although our armed forces are in great need of good, moral leaders to serve, the political arena is also a battlefield in which we must be actively engaged.

On August 18, 1790, President George Washington wrote in a letter to the Yeshuat Israel, Touro Synagogue, penning these words to the members there:

> If we have wisdom to make the best use of the advantages with which we are now favored, we cannot fail, under the just administration of a good Government, to become a great and a happy people ... May the Father of all mercies scatter light and not darkness in our paths, and make us all in our several vocations useful here, and in His own due time and way, everlastingly happy.[71]

Does My Vote Even Count?

A common question many people have about the political process is: Does my vote even count? "I'm just one of millions," they say, "so what does it matter? Isn't our election process rigged? My vote won't change the outcome anyway."

The false belief that "my vote doesn't really count" is more of a fallacy when you look at local races. The first race my husband ran was for a State Representative seat. He was challenging a ten-year incumbent who had been a county sheriff, and it was a tough race. He won that race by 249 votes, and believe me, every vote counted! Just do a search online for some state and local elected offices and you will see that they are often decided by a very thin margin, sometimes less than twenty-five votes.

Let's dive into some facts about this issue.

Back in the 2000 presidential election, the outcome was uncertain due to recounts taking place in Florida. I remember watching the news and seeing video of long tables in huge rooms where elections staff and poll workers were helping to hand count each ballot. The image of one man holding a ballot up to the light trying to determine if he could see a "hanging chad" in every news report and newspaper. The people at those tables, counting the ballots in those key Florida counties, were playing a critical role in a presidential election. It made me think about something I hadn't ever thought of before.

The people counting the ballots had to get into those positions somehow. Had they run for the position? Were they volunteers? It just took a little research to learn how different states run their elections. The process differs from state to state, but almost every state relies on volunteer poll workers. There are also local election boards, the County Clerk position, and the Clerk's office staff. They are involved in making sure the ballot counting is done correctly and transparently in their county. Of course, the Secretary of State is the top elected state official responsible for overseeing the elections in each state.

You can find more information about the election process at this website: https://usafacts.org/articles/how-are-votes-counted/.[72]

There has been great concern about election integrity and the influence of foreign actors and ballot manipulation in recent elections. It is a valid concern. The folklore surrounding certain areas of Chicago, Philadelphia, counties in Ohio and Michigan, and other places around the country is widespread. The foreign actors who would do anything to bring our country down have been involved in trying to influence the races for Secretary of State, Attorney General, or even regional prosecutor's races.

These are all valid concerns and real threats to our elections, but the best way to ensure that our elections are secure is for every God-fearing American to follow the guidelines laid out in the next few chapters for being effectively engaged in the political process. We the people must be engaged, involved, and vigilant. If we work to elect the right people to state offices such as the Secretary of State, the Attorney General, the local prosecutor, the school board, and every position up and down the ballot, we will not only put guardians of liberty in office, but we will have a connection to those elected officials which allows us to hold them accountable in many ways.

Am I Even Qualified?

The requirement for eligibility to serve in any of those positions is not as demanding as you might think. Volunteering to work the polls requires a day of training, an early morning arrival the day of the election, and a long day of work, but the fact that you will be helping to secure the votes of every member of your community should make it worth a little sacrifice for two days. There are also polling place observers, sent by each political party, to ensure that the rules and laws for elections are followed by those working the polls.

As my father once told me, "You are only responsible for what you know. But you *are* responsible for what you know, and you better do some good with it." Now that *you* know that ballots are counted on the local level first—usually at your local courthouse or county office building—and that there are local positions that must be filled to help ensure that the ballot counting is done correctly, what are you going to do about it? Will you volunteer to work the polls? Will you run for County Clerk? If so, keep in mind that there are conferences and training schools for those who are elected to the County Clerk position, in case it seems a little too intimidating.

The Front Lines of Politics Are Local

Why are local and state positions important? It's simple. When someone is elected to a school board position and they have done a good job, do they sometimes run for county commissioner or county council? Yes. If they do a good job as a member of the county council, and they have developed good name recognition in the community, do they sometimes run for state representative? Yes. When a state representative has served for a good amount of time and has had experience crafting and passing legislation on the state level, do they sometimes run for US Congress? Yes.

When someone runs for a local office, that opens up the possibility that they might run for the next level of public service. Which brings up another very important point about why your vote counts and why researching the candidates all the way down the ballot is so important.

Party Positions

Another way to be involved is to run for or be appointed as a delegate to the state party convention. Each party has a state convention and a national convention. These conventions will debate and vote on the official positions of the various parties. This is an important place to be. Many times, the Secretary of State candidates and other statewide offices will be elected as the party candidate at these conventions before running against the other nominees across the state. The Secretary of State is a vital position. They safeguard the election process to keep every vote and polling place secure.

Being a delegate to the state party convention was an honor for me and one of the most interesting and encouraging experiences I have had in politics. At one convention, there were some people in the party leadership who wanted to make some changes to the party's position on traditional marriage. They wanted to remove the language stating support for traditional marriage and replace it with language that was more vague.

Those who were pushing for the change knew that they would have to have a vote by the entire convention, and so they gathered some young people and those members who were supporting their effort and gave them little handheld noisemakers and whistles. They told them that when the vote was called on the new language, they should make as much noise as possible to make their numbers seem larger than they were. Thankfully, the majority of delegates got wind of this plan and the secretary of the party who was running the meeting decided not to do an audible vote, but a standing vote. A standing vote would mean that when you wanted to vote for something, you would stand and be counted.

The time for the vote came. The new, vague language on the issue of marriage was put on the screen for all to read. The Secretary called for all those in favor to please stand. The supporters stood, blowing whistles and making a lot of noise by cheering and using their noise makers. Finally, the Secretary asked them to be seated. Then, the Secretary put the existing language in support of traditional marriage on the screen for all to read. He asked for all of those in favor of the existing language to remain in the platform to please stand. Silently, without a single noise, a huge majority stood to their feet. It was a powerful statement from the "silent majority," and it was heard loud and clear. I talked to many who witnessed it, and without exception, every one of them was thankful that they had run as a delegate and thankful that they had been there to be counted. Every vote counts!

Understanding the Issue of Life in the Post-Roe Era

On June 24, 2022, the Supreme Court of the United States handed down a landmark decision in Dobbs vs. Jackson, which essentially overruled two previous decisions, Roe. vs. Wade (1973) and Planned Parenthood vs. Casey (1992). The Supreme Court ruled in 2022 that the US Constitution does *not* confer the right to abortion, and the court returned the power to regulate any aspect of abortion not protected by federal law back to the individual states. This changed the landscape of the pro-life vs. abortion debate.

When the Supreme Court hands down a ruling, it is sometimes applied in such a way that an existing law is reversed or a new policy is enacted. Such was the case with the Supreme Court's decision on the legality of abortion in the case of Roe vs. Wade. As with other issues, because of the recent Dobbs decision, the federal policy regarding pre-born life and the legality of abortion was reversed after fifty years, and the issue was sent back to the states for the most part. The issue must now be determined by individual state legislatures and so there will be differing approaches to the legality of abortion across the country. This does not mean that Congress can't take any more action on the pro-life issue. In fact, there is still much work to be done on both the state and federal levels.

Answering the Critics

The issue of protecting life is not just about pre-born life. Critics of those who are pro-life have accused them of only caring about pre-born children but not caring for them after they are born. There are many aspects to the pro-life movement that have been happening without much media attention, but that have made a difference in thousands of lives. They have built thousands of pregnancy resource centers to counsel young mothers about their pregnancy, provide them with childcare, and help them find a job, housing, and many other things after the baby is born. They have established adoption agencies, hosted diaper drives and food bank efforts, and supported those in need in their communities.

There is still much to do on the legislative front regarding the issue of life. Adoption is still expensive and difficult, religiously affiliated adoption agencies have been under attack by the woke agenda, our foster care system is in much need of reform, and single mothers need help and support from their communities in many ways. The legal and financial problems caused by state and federal regulations in all of these areas could be addressed and corrected. Protecting life means all life, and those who desire to help children in need of adoption or struggling single mothers should not be handcuffed by regulation and unreasonable restrictions from the government. If you remember our analogy, the three-legged stool is useless when one leg is larger than the others. Each must be kept to its proper size and function.

The Question Pro-Life Americans Must Answer

So here is my question for you: Is abortion illegal in America now?

The answer is: No. It is still legal in some states, and it is only illegal at varying degrees, depending on the state. Because of the Dobbs decision, issues regarding pre-born life and the legality of abortion must now be determined by individual state legislatures. If you have further interest in the current state of the pro-life/abortion debate, please visit the Susan B. Anthony Pro-Life Action for America website for the latest information at https://sbaprolife.org.

Why All Issues Matter at Every Level

With that in mind, ask yourself this question: If you are voting to elect a person to a school board position, is it important to know their stance on the issue of life and abortion? If your answer is yes, you are right! It matters now more than ever!

"But," you argue, "they won't be dealing with abortion decisions as a school board member."

True. Although school board members are mainly handling millions of dollars of education funding from the state and federal levels as well as determining school policies on a variety of issues, they usually don't deal with the pro-life issue. And yet, if you don't research the candidate's stance on that issue when they are running for school board, once they are elected, they develop good name recognition and people get used to seeing their name on the ballot. Then, when they decide to run for state representative, it will be harder to defeat them at that point. If they were pro-abortion when they served on the school board, they will be pro-abortion when they run for state representative, where they will be making decisions on that issue.

The lesson we must all keep in mind is this: we must vet candidates at every level on every key issue that matters to us because their election to that first lower-level position usually leads them to the next level of service. Once they are in an elected position, it is harder to beat them when they run for the next position. In politics, this is called the power of incumbency. The power of incumbency includes the ability of an elected official to develop name recognition in the community, to hold fundraisers, and to keep a campaign bank account which can usually be used toward the next campaign in some way. It also includes the fact that they have established a campaign team, a group of volunteers, a marketing strategy, relationships with members of the media through interviews, a record to run on, and much more.

The Power of Incumbency & Vetting the Candidates

Over the years, the power of incumbency has grown in its effectiveness in politics. This is why we see people in Congress who stay in office and keep getting elected term after term. Many have been there for twenty years or more, and a major factor in their longevity is the power of incumbency. Their constituents get used to voting for them, develop a familiarity with their record, and become somewhat loyal to them as their representative.

The principle of vetting candidates at the lower levels is extremely important. You may know the guy running for commissioner will never run for mayor, but strange things happen in politics. You never know where a candidate will end up some day, and if you don't vet them in that first campaign and make sure that they hold your same worldview, by the time they have served for several years in office, they will have the power of incumbency.

You also never know when an issue that is important to you will become a local issue, and if you haven't elected people who hold your same values and beliefs, you will be dealing with things you could not have imagined would become problems.

During the 2020 Covid crisis, my husband and I were running a property that had been a tourist attraction for over fifty years. When the governor began issuing executive orders with protocols and limitations for public spaces, the local health departments were put in charge of making decisions about whether or not various businesses could be open and what protocols they would need to implement.

Do you think it was important to us, as small business owners, that we had good people in those positions who would work with us and be committed to protecting constitutionally protected rights? You bet! We worked with our local sheriff's department and county commissioners as well. Each and every local position is critical in an election—not just president.

Here is a website that lists voter registration deadlines for all fifty states and links to registration websites: www.ivotevalues.org.

Make Sure to Register!

Many states allow you to register to vote at the local Department of Motor Vehicles or Bureau of Motor Vehicles. Once you are registered, you will want to know who is on the ballot and what offices are up for election. Here is a good source for that:

https://ballotpedia.org/Sample_Ballot_Lookup.

According to the American National Election Study, in 1990, Americans were almost evenly split, 50-50, when asked if there were important differences between the two mainline political parties. In 2020, the study revealed a huge shift in that same view, reporting that 90 percent of Americans believed that there were important differences between the two mainline political parties.[73] What changed? How has our view of the two parties become so divided so fast?

When you talk to your friends and neighbors, do you agree on the majority of basic life values like family, community, service, and faith? Do you agree that tax dollars should be used wisely? Do you agree that corruption from any elected official should not be tolerated and that all children deserve the chance for a quality education in a safe and nurturing community? The majority of us would answer with a resounding, "Yes."

But there is a major change happening in our culture right now, and it would be wise to know where the political parties stand on issues that matter to us. Again, choosing to vote for a particular party does not mean that you have to be "sold out" to everything that party does. But in our political system, it is important that we are informed on the issues and that we make the best choice possible when voting for a candidate.

At the back of the book is a section of excerpts taken directly from the 2023 official national platforms for the two largest political parties, with links to websites of the platforms of other parties.

The party platforms are agreed to and voted on at the national conventions every four years, but because of the pandemic in 2020, some agreed to extend the existing platforms from 2016. Each state party adopts its own platform as well. Please read through these national platforms carefully and decide which party best represents your values and worldview. Links to the full platforms are provided as well.

I cannot emphasize enough how important it is for you to turn to these pages and read through the excerpts I have provided. It will help you tremendously to understand the differences and which way you lean politically on various issues.

CHAPTER TEN

AN EASY HOW-TO GUIDE FOR BECOMING POLITICALLY ACTIVE - NOW!

After reading through the excerpts from the different platforms, I encourage you to take some time to pray about which party best represents your faith, values, and priorities as you consider the choices you make in electing leaders for our nation.

Also, please keep this important fact in mind: There has never been, nor will there ever be, a perfect candidate or a perfect party. Some candidates who sound so good to you on the campaign trail can end up being a disappointment on an a particular issue or even overall. Once you have helped with a campaign or cast your vote in the election, make sure that you try to keep up with the actions that each official takes while in office. You can do this by going to your state government website and choosing their office title or doing a search for their name.

Sadly, when you do a web search for a candidate's name, there will sometimes be articles presenting negative things about them, especially if the candidate has run in a divisive race or has served in office before. It is astounding how the corporate media complex can twist facts, use partial truths, and even completely fabricate stories in order to spread lies and take a political opponent down.

I have personally experienced this with members of the media. I have given interviews and then watched the report they give, and I have been shocked at how the reporter cherry-picked my words, presented me in the worst light possible, or misrepresented what I actually said. I have woken up to read news headlines and articles which I knew for a fact were completely false, and the sad thing is that candidates do not have any recourse to correct false stories. Stories used to be printed in newspapers and then they would be all but forgotten after the election. Now, with the advent of the internet, the stories stay around forever.

I know one elected official who was asked if a certain policy was decided in a meeting he had attended, and recorded himself answering with a definitive "no." The reporter pushed further, and the official emphasized that what the reporter was insinuating happened simply didn't happen. Using misleading words and omitting certain facts, the reporter proceeded to write a story that was completely fabricated. When the elected official saw the story, he called back and asked the reporter why he had written such a fabrication, and the reporter's response was stunning. He said that if he was right, he would be praised for being the first to break the story, and if he was wrong, there was nothing anyone could do about it.

I have seen candidates send cease and desist letters to news outlets because of false stories that they spread, but that is the limit to what a candidate can do until they are out of office. The news media and many campaign participants who desire position and power over anything else, simply do not care what they do to their opponent's reputation. In fact, I have heard this mantra repeated by professional politicos and campaign workers alike: Make up stories until something sticks, as long as it takes the political opponent down.

So make it a point to do thorough research from sources that you trust, and whenever possible, meet the candidate in person. Ask them about the issues that matter most to you. Assess them face to face, watch their actions, see how they and their family conduct themselves in the community, and make your own decision based on your own observations.

Staying Informed, Engaged and Involved

As a citizen, your job is not over after you cast your ballot on election day. Holding elected officials accountable for their actions or lack of actions while in office is an important and sacred duty of an engaged citizen. This is part of the problem with our political system today. For too long we have believed the lie that if we vote for the right party or the right person, then we have done our part.

As I stated in the preface to the book, we are all human, and this is a human system of government. We will never be in perfect agreement on everything, but those who are elected should stay in alignment with the basic values for which they were elected. If they make a mistake or fail on an issue, but the majority of their other actions are consistent with what you believe, don't obsess over their one failure and forget to appreciate the majority of actions that they get right. Remember President Ronald Reagan's 80/20 rule!

Ways to Help in a Campaign

There are many ways you can help a political campaign and it can be something the whole family can enjoy. A campaign manager is in charge of organizing all aspects of the campaign. From the calendar of events to email lists, the campaign manager oversees all the facets of the organization. Here are some easy ways you could help on a campaign:

1. **Offer to host a fundraiser** at your house and invite your friends, neighbors, and business associates. This does not require a lot of work. You will need to set a date for the candidate to come, and then you will usually be

given invitations to either mail or email. Candidates can accept donations in the form of food and refreshments, which is called an in-kind donation, so if you provide food or pay for catering, you can offer to pay for it as an in-kind donation to the campaign. This can be a very informal gathering in your living room or on your patio. Have light finger foods and drinks, and the campaign will provide material to put out for people to read. You might be asked to share why you support the candidate, and then the candidate will speak and take questions. There will usually be someone who is in charge of taking the donations that people bring, and they will let people know if there are any limits on donations and who they should make the checks out to, etc.

2. **Offer web design and logo design services.** If this is your area of expertise, candidates are always looking for help with these. They can pay you for your work, or you can work out an agreement regarding the amount of time you will donate as an in-kind donation and the amount they will pay you to do further work on top of that.

3. **Run phone banks.** Sometimes campaigns will set aside days for a group of volunteers to make phone calls to voters. There is usually a simple script with different options for you to use when talking to voters. It is easy and can be very fun when you do it with friends. This also helps to identify addresses for yard sign placements.

4. **Put out yard signs.** Campaigns always need help putting out yard signs. When they have specific addresses which have agreed to put out a yard sign, they will need someone to drive to the various locations and put them up. The night before the election, most polling places allow candidates to put their signs outside the polling place in certain areas. This takes time, so having volunteers put signs at polling places the night before the

election is very helpful. They will also need help driving around the district to take the yard signs down the day after the election.

5. **Walk in parades or work** a booth at a festival. The whole family can have fun putting on campaign T-shirts and walking in parades for the candidate. Wear walking shoes, bring water and snacks, and prepare for a fun time with the campaign crew. Kids can sometimes bring their bikes or ride on a float—whatever the candidate decides to enter in the parade.

6. **Donate door prizes.** If you own a retail business, restaurant or make crafts or unique items, campaigns are always looking for door prizes to give away. You might be able to make a unique craft that makes a great door prize!

7. **Go door to door.** Going door to door for a candidate can be fun for the whole family as well. It usually involves some instruction before you go, maps, and addresses of an area that needs to be canvassed and handing out literature. It's a great way to get to know the people in your community and many times it can be a very encouraging experience.

8. **Watching the legislative process.** Many state legislatures are now live streaming their committee meetings and legislative sessions. Anyone can log on, and watch the committee testimonies, floor debates and votes. Taking the time to follow a bill that interests you or that your representative has authored is a great way to learn about the process and understand the work your representative is doing.

This will require sacrifice on your part. Taking the time to watch votes or track legislative content will take effort and research. You will need to find government websites that provide bill tracking and vote tracking. If you don't have time for this, I would recommend at least signing up for email updates from your local and state officials. They send regular updates on bills that they are supporting and usually provide links to more information about upcoming votes and debates.

I know one very special lady who has helped do all of the suggestions listed above, and because she reads the bills that interest her and has a personal relationship with her representatives, they will call her for advice. They will even call her to let her know that they might be voting a certain way on a bill that she might not like but want to explain why they are voting that way, since they know she will probably be asking them about the vote later. That is an example of a citizen doing their due diligence and holding their representatives accountable.

The Time to Withdraw Support

When choosing to withdraw support from a candidate or elected official, please be careful to base your decision on facts and information you have gathered personally from experience or from documented evidence and not from hearsay. It is amazing how many emotionally driven or illogical reasons people give when deciding whether or not to support a candidate. You should have your own list of important issues and stances that you look for in a candidate, but please make sure your list is not based on whether or not the candidate has a nice website or gives a good stump speech at an event. Listen carefully for their worldview, their philosophy about business and governance, and their reasons for running. Have they spent their entire lives checking off boxes in order to climb the political ladder of position and power? Or have they built a business and raised their children only to find frustration and disappointment with government overreach and limitations of freedom? When an elected official has a proven record of standing for your values and taking action on issues that you believe in, don't abandon them if you find that they disagree on one issue and disappoint you with a vote if the majority of their service has been good. The exception to the rule would be if the elected official has failed in an area that is directly related to the Constitution or the Bill of Rights, or that is a clear overreach of the power given to their office. These issues are fundamental to our liberties, and any action that goes against them cannot and should not be tolerated.

Congressman Crockett's Constitutional Lesson

One example of keeping Constitutional tabs on elected officials is a story recounted by Congressman David (Davy) Crockett of Tennessee who served three terms in Congress in the early 1800s. He was a huge advocate for the poor and giving equal opportunity to all, so it might surprise you that in the Congressional record of 1828 he voted against a proposal to give financial assistance to the widow of a military officer who had died an untimely death, leaving her almost destitute. Congressman Thomas Chilton, who later helped Crockett write his autobiography, joined Crockett in speaking out against the measure at the time. Later, Crockett and Chilton, with the help of author Edward S. Ellis, explained in the 1884 memoir, *Life of Colonel David Crockett,* the reasoning for Crockett's vote against sending the financial assistance.[74]

The record of the Debates in Congress for Wednesday, April 2, 1828, does not have a verbatim record of the speech given by Crockett regarding the motion, but it does record that Congressman Crockett delivered "his sentiments in opposition to the principle of the bill" and that he even made the offer of donating "his quota [paycheck] in his private character [personally], to make up the sum proposed."[75]

His reasoning, as explained in subsequent speeches, articles, and books, was that the proposed financial assistance for the Widow Brown was unconstitutional. He was all for helping the poor and supporting the great service of the military, and he was one of the most outspoken advocates for the common man, but he drew the line at spending money beyond the limited bounds of Congressional allowances in the Constitution. This principle he claimed to have learned the hard way, from a constituent who refused to support his re-election to Congress.

In his autobiography, Crockett shared what he told his Congressional colleagues during the debate. Keep in mind that Col. David Crockett was known for being a great storyteller and would sometimes exaggerate things to make the point of an important principle. Some have doubted the veracity of the story, but his vote against the measure is verified by the Congressional record, and his story of a conversation he had with a Tennessee farmer is not so far-fetched that it is not believable. The principle of what Crockett presents in the story speaks to the importance of citizens doing their due diligence and holding our elected officials accountable—especially when it comes to the Constitution.

Crockett recounts that while traveling his district, a constituent told him that he couldn't vote for him for re-election because he believed Crockett's view of the Constitution was different from his own. He had based his conclusion on a vote that Crockett had made which authorized sending a special amount of money to help those affected by a fire near Washington. Crockett argued that a difference in opinion over one vote should not constitute a removal from office. The voter countered with the fact that the underlying principle of the vote revealed Crockett's disregard for the Constitution and the limits on Congressional powers.

Crockett said the answer changed his perspective as a member of Congress on the power of the purse. The constituent stated that "the Constitution, to be worth anything, must be held sacred, and rigidly observed in all its provisions. The man who wields power and misinterprets it, is the more dangerous the more honest he is ... For when Congress once begins to stretch its power beyond the limits of the Constitution, there is no limit to it, and no security for the people."[74]

With the help of his biographer, Ellis, he shared what he said to his Congressional colleagues:

> We have the right, as individuals, to give away as much of our own money as we please in charity; but as members of Congress we have no right so to appropriate a dollar of the public money. I am the poorest man on this floor. I cannot vote for this bill, but I will give one week's pay to the object, and if every member of Congress will do the same, it will amount to more than the bill asks.[74]

A Healthy Debate

Our system was created to encourage opposing sides of an issue to come to the table, engage in a healthy, respectful debate, and present their case to those factually and logically. It is a sometimes tedious process. Many different voices will have the right to weigh in and to suggest changes to improve the idea. They will offer warnings regarding future consequences or estimated results of the bill, if it is enacted. Then there will be multiple votes on the bill by the elected officials

When a legislator proposes a law, it is passed through what I like to call a series of governmental filters, including the following steps:

1. An initial legal consultation and analysis
2. Committee deliberation in both legislative bodies
3. Amendment changes in committees and in both legislative bodies
4. At least four to six rounds of debates and subsequent votes by the full body of the legislature.

Then it is passed on to the governor or president to sign into law. If the executive branch does not want to sign it, they have the option to veto the bill. The legislature then has the opportunity to override the veto, but that takes a huge effort to accomplish.

Does this sound tedious and time-consuming? It is! Passing a law is a long and difficult process, and that is a very good thing! If it were easy to pass a law, we would be strapped with so many laws we probably couldn't even function as a free society.

Be Careful and Respectful

Before calling out an elected official publicly for voting the wrong way on legislation, make sure you have up-to-date information. Passing a law is a long process, and bills can change throughout the process.

I remember one instance during my husband's third week in Congress, when a person who had supported his campaign received some wrong information about a bill which was moving through Congress. The person had worked with our team and had my husband's personal cell phone and email address. We made it a point to be reachable and available to those on our campaign team so that they could ask questions, keep him accountable, and help get accurate information.

However, this person read somewhere in an online forum that he had voted the "wrong way" on a bill and immediately sent out an email to a large list, claiming he had "gone Washington" and betrayed their trust. The problem was, my husband had actually voted the "right" way and the information had been inaccurate. If this person had called or emailed to confirm the information, we could have provided a link showing them the record of the vote. As a result, my husband's personal email and text message service was so overloaded with messages that his device completely shut down and he could not access it for several days.

This person had direct access to their elected official but never took the time to even ask—by text, email or phone call—if the report they had read "somewhere" was true or not. Needless to say, this did not go over well with my husband or with me. It was hurtful and served as a good reminder that we must all be careful to take the time to get accurate, documented information before jumping to conclusions. The moral of the story? When you have direct access to the source, use it!

When contacting your officials, please keep the following things in mind:

1. Know the facts before you make contact. When you approach an elected official about an issue, do your research as much as possible before you talk to them to discuss your concerns.

2. Be open to answers that might surprise you due to the ever-changing legislative process. As we have learned, the lawmaking process is slow and convoluted. Proposed bills are amended, changed, and even withdrawn as they work their way through committees. Ask them where a bill stands in the process first.

3. Bring useful data to the table. If you have had personal experience with an issue, write it down and bring your personal experience as an example as to why you think the policy should be changed, or the law will create unnecessary paperwork, or whatever your experience has been.

4. Remember that the advantage you have when approaching an elected official is that you are a constituent, not a paid lobbyist. Your vote and support holds much more sway and influence with the official than a paid lobbyist—or at least it should!

The Marks of Servant Leadership

I want to elaborate a little more on that last point. As a former state legislator and being married to a former state and federal legislator, I believe that constituent services should be the top priority of any elected representative of the people. If you run for office, always put the people you serve as your first priority. You should never be too busy to talk to a constituent who takes the time to seek you out about an issue.

A good representative will value and invite input from constituents more than any paid lobbyist or special interest group. In fact, I personally had many constituents' contact information—people I knew personally—for the express purpose of reaching out to them on a regular basis to ask their opinions and input on a variety of issues.

Elected officials will never know everything about every subject, regardless of how much they study and apply themselves. I am not a banker, I am a former teacher, author, small business owner, and composer. Banking was not my expertise. I valued the opinions of people in my district who lived and breathed the banking industry every day and who could weigh in on issues that affected their businesses.

Sure, the banks had lobbyists and bankers' associations, but I preferred hearing directly from my actual constituents at our local banks to know exactly how proposed laws would affect them directly. The same would go for every other business sector—agriculture, manufacturing, education, healthcare, etc.

The most important reason that serving constituents should be the number one priority of a public servant is that every elected official is employed by the people to serve the people. The people pay the salary and are the employer of any public servant.

Staying Connected with Elected Officials

As you become more engaged in politics, try to give your contact information to any elected officials you meet and let them know your work sector, experience, and expertise. They need sources in their district whom they know and trust when they need honest answers on a variety of issues.

The Power of the People

I will never forget a rally that was held at the state house when my husband was serving his first term in office. Hundreds of young mothers with small children had received word that a bill was being considered which would put even more of a burden on them as mothers, and they were not happy about it! One mom had kept tabs on the bill and she had contacted all of her friends. They organized quickly and planned a rally at the state house on the day it was going to be heard in committee. They all had to rearrange their schedules and take time away from their normal commitments in order to take the day to lobby their legislators.

I watched as hundreds of moms hauled strollers and car seats and diaper bags and lunch boxes into the Capitol building. They had to reserve the space ahead of time and make arrangements to get a microphone and speakers and a stage. They carried homemade signs, and some even had made some little handouts to give to legislators.

It was amazing to watch the faces of those state legislators seeing this huge gathering of moms on a mission filling the state house. Boy, were those legislators curious, as well as looking a little nervous and a bit concerned! These ladies were *not* paid lobbyists. These were moms—angry moms—from the legislator's own districts, and they had taken time out of their crazy busy schedules, toddlers in tow, to express their concerns about a proposed bill. This got the attention of everyone in the state house!

How to "Lobby" Your Legislator

We have all heard about the lobbyists in Washington and in our state capitols. They are paid by business associations or a variety of groups to stand in the lobby of the legislature and talk to as many legislators as they can about the issues that their association is concerned about. Sometimes they provide lunch or invite them to presentations where they share their concerns about bills or ideas for possible solutions to problems related to their business.

When you have an issue you wish to discuss with your representative, you are allowed to lobby your legislator! In fact, you are the most powerful lobbyist that a legislator can meet with. You aren't paid to do it. You are their employer, and you have every right to share your concerns and ideas with them. You can go to the state house or contact them personally and talk to them about what you think they should do on an issue. Just keep in mind, you will need to gather all of the facts and get as much current information as possible on the issue as well as the status of the legislation.

A Citizen's Approach to Lobbying

If you decide to lobby your legislator, do it respectfully and in an organized way. I have seen groups of citizens bring their legislators handmade crafts, small state-themed pieces of art with the state flag or emblems, and even homemade baked goods wrapped in beautiful plastic bags with handwritten notes tied to them. Sometimes a simple thank you note goes a long way!

When you need to talk to your elected official, I would highly recommend bringing ideas for solutions to the problem you want to address and not just complaints about problems. To be perfectly blunt, the majority of communications that legislators receive from their constituents are complaints. It is very rare for a legislator to receive an idea or a solution to a problem.

When I met with constituents, I would always ask them for advice, ideas, or even possible solutions to the problems they were bringing to me. That approach really fostered a constructive conversation on the issue. The points that my constituents made always gave me ideas for ways to solve the problem or to resolve their concerns legislatively.

Remember the Spouse and Family of the Candidate or Official

From the perspective of the spouse of the elected official, please keep in mind that when you meet the candidate or elected official, and their spouse is present, make it a point to talk to them as well. I can't tell you how many times I have felt invisible in a room because everyone was vying for the attention of my husband, to get his opinion or share their concerns with him. Please make sure to acknowledge the spouse and try to share a genuine, positive appreciation for their sacrifice and service as well. And don't forget the children! The family of the official goes through a lot of things behind the scenes that they aren't at liberty to share, but that can be very difficult. Kind words from a constituent go further than you can ever imagine!

After touring the Suffragette House, just a couple blocks from the US Capitol building in Washington D.C., I found it very interesting that Susan B. Anthony, Elizabeth Cady Stanton, Alice Paul, and the many women who lobbied Congress for a woman's right to vote took great pains to get to know the wives of the members of Congress. Although the wives could not vote, the suffragettes knew how influential a spouse could be behind the scenes. The leaders of the women's suffrage movement took time to visit with Congressional wives and even became very close friends with many of them. They showed appreciation for their service and understood the influence that a good spouse can have in the life of an elected official.

Practical Tips to Keep in Mind

So you are now a registered voter, you have studied the party platforms, you know the names of the people on your ballot, and you are familiar with the roles and duties of the offices they are seeking. There are several options for your next steps.

I. Research the candidates by reading their positions on their websites, social media, or a neutral, fact-based website.

> Once you know their positions on the issues that are important to you, you should:

>> A. Choose the candidate closest to your values.
>> B. Make plans to contact the candidates directly.
>> C. Attend a local event where you can meet the candidates in person.

Please keep in mind, it is *easy* for a candidate to do some polling, find out what people want to hear, and then formulate a speech stating their support for what the people support. When choosing a candidate, look at their *actions and not just their words*!

Here are a few of the questions I have listed as my personal priorities when deciding which candidates to support:

1. Are they open about their faith? Do they give clear, concise answers about their personal faith, their church, and their convictions?
2. Do they say they are pro-life? If they do, have they attended local pro-life dinners or helped the local crisis pregnancy center in some way? Have they served on the board of a pro-life organization or have they attended a march for life in their town or even in Washington, DC?
3. Do they say they are pro-business? If so, have they ever actually run a business? Or have they always taken paycheck from an employer or the government? If they have never had to make payroll, how can they understand the

direct effect that regulations, high taxation, and inflation have on small business owners?

4. Do they support parental rights and school choice laws? If so, what is their record on those issues?

5. Do they say they are pro Second Amendment? If so, do they mean they are for allowing guns for hunters only? What actions have they taken to protect Second Amendment issues? Do they personally own guns? When I ask them, how well do they articulate the truth of the Founders' reasons for authoring the Second Amendment?

II. Sign-up for the candidate's email updates and like them on social media.

    A. Through those avenues, they will announce locations for public meetings, fundraisers, rallies, parades etc.

    B. Make your plans to meet them at one of their events and bring a list of questions to ask them.

    C. You can also help promote them by posting positive comments, posting links to positive news reports, and sharing information about upcoming public events they will be attending or hosting.

III. You can volunteer for their campaign by finding contact information for their campaign manager.

    A. Developing a good rapport with the campaign manager is very important, not just during the campaign.

    B. When the candidate is in office, the campaign manager will still be a key person to help you hold that persona accountable and follow the voting record or actions taken by the person you helped elect.

C. They will also connect you with other people on the campaign team who hold your same beliefs and worldview.

IV. Here are a few more ways you could become more informed and engaged:

A. Volunteer to walk in parades, work a booth at festivals, attend door to door drives, help work on phone banks, etc.

B. Know the facts before you make contact. When you call the campaign team, be well informed on their platform and issues as well as current local issues that might be on the agenda.

C. Offer to provide material or money for parade handouts like candy or little toys for kids.

D. Offer to provide handmade crafts for the campaign to use as door prizes at dinners and events.

E. Offer to start a prayer team for the campaign.

F. Volunteer to set up the candidate table and materials at festivals, fairs, fundraising events, and other public gatherings where they need people to hand out information.

G. Offer to host a coffee or reception at your home and invite your neighbors, friends, and family.

H. Offer to write a letter to the editor or send out a personal email to all of your friends and family sharing why you are supporting the candidate.

I. Offer to help with a fundraiser at your home or at a local restaurant.

J. Ask what campaign materials they need: T-shirts for volunteers, logo design, website design, palm cards, banners, yard signs, etc.

V. Consider running for an elected position. If that is what you decide, you will need to take the following steps:

    A. Assess the need.

        1. Who is running for that position?

        2. Are they doing a good job?

        3. Do they represent your values?

        4. What is their record?

    E. Consider the qualifications.

        1. What does the job require?

        2. Are you qualified and experienced in the area that the office will deal with most?

    C. Find a campaign school and plan to attend. There are many that are offered:

        1. Farm Bureau Candidate Training

        2. State House Campaign School

        3. Conservative organizations' training seminars

    D. Fundraising.

        1. Are you willing to work to raise the amount of money needed to run a good campaign?

        2. Research how much money was spent on the last campaign for the position you are considering and factor that amount into your plans.

        3. Make a list of your network of business associates, family, friends, etc. in the community who would donate to your campaign.

D. Decide on your platform.
  1. Why are you running?
  2. What actions will you take if elected?
  3. What issues are most important to you?
  4. What is your record or position regarding those issues?

E. Remember your faith.
  1. In elected office, your faith should inform your decisions.
  2. You should be up front and clear about your faith from the outset, so that people know where you stand and how your faith will guide your decision making, if elected.

C. Dismiss the title. The title belongs to the *people*!
  1. Remember that whatever position you seek, the title is only temporary.
  2. If you are elected, that title of commissioner or mayor or representative or senator belongs to the people! It is not yours. You are a temporary steward of that title until the next person is elected to hold that position.
  3. Don't allow the title to become a part of who you are as a person.

  Please be warned: Once your identity becomes attached to the title and position, you will make yourself more susceptible to compromise. When people know you will do anything to keep the title because your identity is reliant on that title, they will be able to threaten you with finding someone to run against you "unless you compromise." This will happen slowly, but more and more on issues that are important to you.

CHAPTER ELEVEN

A QUICK GUIDE TO THE LEGISLATURE

As I mentioned in the beginning of this book, by the time I was married, I could have used a refresher course on civics! In this chapter I want to provide you with a quick overview of the legislative process so you understand how a bill becomes law and how you can be effective in advocating for the causes that you believe in. So, here we go!

The majority of state legislatures are made up of two groups of elected representatives:

1. The House of Representatives
2. The Senate

They meet in the capital city of the state in their respective chambers. Many state capitol buildings house both legislative bodies, but some meet in separate buildings. I knew a state senator who used to tease members of the House of Representatives by saying, "You know, we are the 'upper house,' better known as, the 'House of Lords' and you are the 'lower house,' better known as the 'House of Commons.'" That always got a laugh and started a debate for sure! The House side has a larger number of members because they represent a smaller area or district than the Senators.

The goal in having the representatives represent smaller areas and be up for reelection every two years is to keep them closer to the people and how policies affect us on a daily basis. The Senate is usually the smaller body, and their districts cover a larger area of the state. Their terms are longer—sometimes four years and sometimes six years—and they are meant to be the more deliberative body. With fewer members and longer terms, they are able to do deeper dives into major issues while still having to work with the House side to pass the state budget, roads funding, and other necessary duties of the state government. The Senate usually focuses more on larger policies and long-term solutions.

The States: The Experimental Labs of Self-Governance

America is unique in that each state has its own state constitution, its own rules for each chamber, and its own legislative calendar. Things differ from state to state, so some state legislatures are part-time and some are full-time.

If your state has a part-time legislature, that means that most, if not all of the State Representatives and State Senators have another full or part-time job in their home districts. That is the way that the US Congress began—as a part-time citizen legislature—where the members would pass laws and then have to go back home and live under the laws they just passed. While they were home working their full-time jobs, they would rub shoulders with their friends and neighbors, be active in their communities, and stay in close contact with their constituents on a regular basis.

The Journey of a Legislator

The legislative process is important for you to understand when trying to address your concerns with your elected representatives. When your representative first arrives at the State House or in Congress, they attend some type of orientation training. This can last anywhere from one to five days. They are given a refresher course on the process of how a bill becomes law, the rules of the legislative body, security issues, expectations for decorum, the electronic devices they will be given, and much more.

After their initial training, they will attend a caucus meeting. Each major party has their own caucus meeting room. The leadership of each party in each chamber will determine where and when their members will meet. The caucus meetings are for elected members only, with the rare exception of allowing a few people who are on staff for the leadership to help with paperwork, run errands, and take notes. These meetings are like a family chat and are highly confidential.

In these caucus meetings, members sometimes have the opportunity to present their proposed bills and discussions are allowed between the members and leadership. There are "priority" bills, such as the state budget, healthcare issues, roads and infrastructure, education funding, etc., which are presented by the leadership team. They have usually worked on crafting the priority bills before the legislative session starts. The priority bills are usually large and take a lot of time to read, understand, and debate in the caucus.

Caucus meetings can also be used to address any inner-party disagreements or to present a new idea that might need more explanation than what is written in the bill. So, the caucus room is a place of confidential debate within the political party membership and usually precedes any committee discussions.

If your representative files a bill, they have done the following:

1. Researched the subject matter and decided that they have a good solution to a problem and decided that this solution will not just work as an amendment to another bill, and that it is worthy of being proposed as a standalone bill and a needed law. Please keep in mind that many times state legislators are allowed to file only a certain number of bills per session.

2. Explained their idea to the state legal counsel department and worked with a lawyer to craft the exact wording that they believe will work best to address the problem.

How A Bill Becomes Law

The next step in the process is to file the bill and make it public. This usually involves approval by the legal department and sometimes the leadership. Once the bill is filed, it will be given a number or a title and will be posted on the legislative website. Then the legislator will begin to "sell" the idea of the bill to the chairman of the committee to which the bill will most likely be assigned. The Speaker of the House determines which bills will be assigned to which committee. The chairman of the committee will be the one to decide whether or not to give the bill a hearing. If the bill has to do with education, the author will go to the Chairman of the Education Committee. If it is a bill having to do with veterans' issues, the author will go to the Chairman of the Veterans Affairs Committee.

If he or she is successful in convincing the chairman to give the bill a hearing, the chairman adds the bill to his list of bills to be heard in the committee. Committee chairmen have a lot on their plate. It is their job to read through all of the bills sent to them by the Speaker, then to determine which bills should be considered by the committee members.

Once the bill is on the list to have a hearing by a committee, your representative is assigned a day when the bill will need to be presented. Before the hearing date, your representative should go to each member of the committee and try to explain the need for the bill. This takes time and an ability to explain complex issues in an effective way. The representative needs to be ready with answers to any kind of concern or question about the bill, so they should be doing a lot of research to make sure that their bill is effective and has been well worded to address the problem.

Let's say that you have talked to your representative about a bill they are proposing, and you are fully supportive of it. You might want to ask them if it would help for you to write a letter of support to the chairman. Many times, legislators will only talk directly to people from their own districts, but a chairman is a little more accustomed to hearing from people from all over the state who are interested in bills which are coming before their specific committee.

The other thing you can do is to contact people you know who live in the districts of the members of the committee and ask them to write letters of support for the bill to their representative. If you have expertise in that area, you can either be asked to testify in the hearing or you can take the initiative to attend the hearing. Many times, you are allowed to put your name on the list of speakers to speak about the bill, but there is no guarantee you will be given time to speak if you are not signed up by the committee deadline. The more a legislator hears from constituents on an issue, the more of a priority it will be for them.

Before the day of the committee hearing, the author can file amendments to the bill if changes are needed, but they must send the amendments to the committee chairman for approval and presentation to the committee. On the day of the hearing, the author presents the bill and any approved amendments to the whole committee. Members of the committee ask questions and make comments. There may be some interested groups who send a representative to speak in support or opposition to the bill as well. The author is allowed to bring in experts and supporters to give testimony in the committee, and there is usually a time limit per speaker. Once testimony is heard, both for and against the bill, the committee members go into deliberation and then call for a vote.

First Reading, Second Reading, Final Passage, and Back Again

If the bill is passed in the committee, it is sent to the whole House or Senate for a "first reading." All members of the legislature are responsible for keeping up with bills that are passed out of committee and will be coming to the floor for first reading votes. They should be reading the bills and talking to the authors for any clarification on the bills. The bills that make it through committee are also presented and discussed in caucus meetings where the author is once again expected to explain the necessity for the bill and answer questions about it.

Other members are allowed to offer amendments to bills if they are passed on the first reading. Out of courtesy and respect, they should approach the author with the reason for their amendment. Sometimes the author has their own amendment and can incorporate their colleagues' ideas into their own amendment fairly easily. Other times, the author agrees to allow another member to offer an amendment to their bill. The bill is sent for a second reading vote and amendments to the bill are voted on. Then the whole chamber votes on the passage of the bill as amended.

Building a Coalition of Support

If the bill passes the second reading vote, it is still up for discussion and it is still alive in the process. At this point or possibly even before, the author needs to start finding a co-sponsor in the other legislative chamber who will sign on to the bill and who will be the author in that chamber's process. Some members work on their bill long before the session begins and will take it to the key people around the state who would be involved in passing it into law. Working on a bill far in advance is not always possible, as issues arise that need to be addressed during a legislative session, but when it is possible, a good legislator will do their due diligence to lay a good foundation for a bill's passage.

The author will also need to talk to the chairman of the committee in the other chamber who will be responsible for giving the bill a hearing. The author must be sure to explain the necessity of the bill so that the chairman in the other legislative chamber understands the intent and purpose of the bill. Before the third vote, there is still a chance for further amendments, and then the bill is voted on in a final passage vote.

A Method to the Madness

If this process seems a tad tedious, it is! But this is all an effort to slow down the passage of laws and ensure that the laws that are passed are carefully and methodically studied to determine whether or not they are needed. There are still a few more steps in the process, so hang in there!

If the bill passes all of that, it is then sent to the other legislative body, and the process starts all over again, beginning with the committee hearing. The sponsoring author in that chamber presents the bill to the committee and is usually joined by the original author. Testimony is heard by that committee, the author answers questions, and then the committee deliberates and votes. If the bill passes out of that committee, it goes to the floor of that chamber for the first reading vote. It goes through the amendment process and two more readings before final passage. If it passes that chamber, it is ordered to "engrossment," meaning that both houses have passed it and it is being sent to the original chamber for concurrence (agreement).

When it reaches this final stage in the process, the title and part of the bill is read again, some time for final debate is allowed, and then it is brought for a vote by all members for final passage. But it isn't a law yet!

The Final Signature

If it passes, the bill is considered enrolled, which means it is added to the list of bills to be signed into law by the governor. Once the governor signs the bill, it then becomes a law!

Whew! There is no doubt that this process is thorough, long, and sometimes grueling, but it is meant to examine every angle of a proposed bill and to filter out any laws that could potentially cause problems or impede the free exercise of the Constitutional rights of citizens.

Federal vs. State

The differences between the legislative process on the state and federal level are basically due to the difference in size and scope of each. Similar to the states, Congress is made up of two legislative bodies— the House of Representatives and the Senate. Please remember that a state representative should be addressed as "Representative Smith" and a member of the US House of Representatives should be addressed as "Congressman Smith." A State Senator is still called "Senator Smith," and so is a federal US Senator.

On the federal level, most members live far away from Washington, so they have to find some type of housing to use while they are working in Washington. Most members are empty nesters, so they find a townhouse or apartment and commute back and forth to their home states. Some members have young families, and in an effort to keep the family together as much as possible, they choose to move the family to DC.

This is a difficult decision for young families. Due to the need to be close to family, keep a consistent routine for the kids, or even sometimes due to the age of the children, most decide to keep the family in their home state and have the spouse who is in Congress commute on weekends to be home with the family. This means that the spouse who is at home usually needs an army to surround them with support and help because the spouse who is serving is gone a lot.

From Thursday evening until Monday morning, the member of Congress tries to fit in family time, attending games or activities for their children as well as visiting with district staff and making campaign stops around the district. Evenings can be filled with local association dinners or political party speaking engagements. It can be exhausting.

When my husband was elected to Congress, our boys were eight years old and four years old. Marlin is such a hands-on dad that he didn't want to miss out on seeing the boys every night for dinner or wrestling with them in the living room. So we made the very difficult decision to move our family to a town just south of Washington, in Alexandria, Virginia—close to George Washington's Mount Vernon. Marlin traveled to our home state every other weekend, and when he did, his staff scheduled meetings for him from 8 am – 9 pm every day.

We traveled home as a family for Christmas break and spring break, then spent the entire summer on our farm. It ended up being a total of around five months at home and seven months in Virginia. I homeschooled the boys part of the time, which gave us more flexibility to go home more often.

Our priority was our family, and with the boys being so young, we wanted them to be a part of everything we were doing. It was important for our family to have dinner together at night, for the boys to have us both there to help with homework, and to attend their sporting events. They were involved in 4-H in the summer and helped on the farm. Marlin coached them in basketball and Little League, and I watched their swim lessons and took them to piano lessons. We believed it was important for them to understand that we were a team, serving our state and nation together. Our future opponents did end up trying to use it against us, but we have never regretted the decision to keep our young family together for a moment.

Always keep in mind that there are usually families involved when a person runs for office. There are sacrifices made by the family of the candidate that the public never sees. Be kind. Be aware. And be careful not to believe everything an opponent or the media says about someone.

This is why I must emphasize again that it is vitally important for us to make an extra effort to meet candidates in person for as many positions as possible. In this day and age, hearing a three-second soundbite or hearing something from a local rumor mill should not be the basis for our decision to vote for or against a candidate. It is our job, as the people who are hiring the candidate, to do a thorough interview on our own and to make our decisions based on facts and personal experience.

Congressional Schedules vs. State House Schedules

The other difference between the US Congress and the state legislature is the different legislative schedules. Congress is a full-time position, and the only breaks that members are given are the August recess—when they have the entire month off—and a few extended weekends like New Year's, spring break, Thanksgiving break, and Easter.

I remember that there were times during a lame duck session (a session where the ruling majority has been voted out and the President has lost reelection) when Congress held votes well into the night on Christmas Eve and all the way through to the end of the year. The outgoing majority was working to pass bills that would support their agenda as much as possible before the new majority took control. It is an ever-changing schedule and is set by the Speaker of the House.

Also, on a personal note, please keep in mind that state legislators do *not* go to Washington to vote or work. Only Congressman and Senators go to Washington. I can't tell you how many times, while serving as a state legislator, that I had someone ask me how I liked working in Washington, DC.

If you aren't really involved in politics much, the different levels can be confusing, but I hope that this quick summary helps to clarify the two different positions.

The Power of Incumbency

As far as the power of incumbency which was addressed earlier in the book, it is more of a factor in federal elections than state level elections, but it is still a factor across the board. For instance, if you were to run for your first elected office, I would not recommend starting out with a campaign against a sitting incumbent in the US Congress. Now, you may be an accomplished business owner with plenty of money to spend on the race and plenty of time to campaign, but if the sitting member of Congress has been in office for even one term, they will have a definite advantage in name recognition, a proven voting record, and a working knowledge of the current issues being addressed. Just be very thorough in your approach to considering which office you will choose to run for in your first attempt at public office.

If you are interested in local issues, consider running for an open seat on the school board, town council, or county commissioner board. Having your eyes on the funding numbers, the budget, the state level requirements, and the issues being addressed at that level will prepare you for being more effective at the next level if you are interested in moving to state issues eventually.

Some Extra Notes

As promised, I have shared some reliable information sources at the end of the book as a place for you to start. These will help you in gathering accurate information regarding America's true history, government records, politics, elected officials, and voting records.

If you have read this entire book, you have laid a good foundation for becoming an informed, engaged, American citizen. As my dad always said, "You are only responsible for what you know. You are not responsible for what you don't know. But you should always use what you know and do something good with it."

A Homeschool Family's Influence in Their Community

When my husband was campaigning, I remember being called by a homeschool mom, asking if he would come speak to her group of homeschool families. We set a date and time and when we arrived, we found she had moved all of the furniture out of her living and dining rooms and had replaced it with fifty chairs or more. She had a gorgeously decorated table along the side wall with incredibly fancy homemade desserts.

She had a podium at the front, and we were welcomed with hugs and smiles and warmth by complete strangers. My husband gave a short presentation about himself and why he was running. He spoke from his heart and the people listened intently. Then they opened it up for questions. The husband of the lady who called us stood up. He was a state trooper and a detective who had been with the state police for many years. He asked, "Can you give us your personal testimony, how you came to know God?"

This was not a normal question that we were used to hearing on the campaign stops. My husband eagerly shared his faith journey and his personal belief in the God of the Bible. He shared his belief in the Creator, the inerrancy of the Scriptures, and his prayer that America would turn back to God. When he was done, the lady of the house had tears in her eyes and so did her husband. They looked at their friends who had gathered and several others were moved to tears as well. The big, strong state trooper stood again and said something I will never forget:

"Well, you just put a face to the person we've been praying for. Many of us here have been meeting for quite a while to pray that God would move in the hearts of people of faith to step forward and run for office. After hearing your testimony, I know that you are one of the nameless, faceless people we have been praying for, for so long. It's great to finally meet you."

Andy and Jodi Lohrman have since become some of our dearest friends and have been co-laborers together with us and others in public service. We have laughed together and cried together, and we have all continued to pray for America. Are you one of nameless, faceless people we have been praying for to step forward and be a light in the political arena?

In Conclusion

Our nation has been a light to the world. We have given hope and help to millions! We have sacrificed and endured hardship and we have kept the faith. Now that you have a better knowledge of our true history, our birthright, and the great responsibility that we have as Americans, I ask you now to stop and pray for God's help and guidance.

The foundations of our beloved nation are starting to crumble beneath our feet.

Humanism, socialism, critical theory, and more have been hacking away at the foundations that were laid at great cost by our previous generations. No longer do we need watchmen on the wall; we need workers on the ground, reinforcing the foundations and rebuilding the wall of faith, renewing the basis of our culture by taking action, stepping into the arena, arming themselves with truth, and speaking it with boldness. We need every able-bodied person of faith to get involved in some way to help right the ship of state before it is too late. With God's help, it will be people of faith and virtue who save America.

Now you know. Now you are responsible. What will you do with what you now know?

If virtue & knowledge are diffused among the people, they will never be enslaved. This will be their great security ... Liberty will not long survive the total extinction of morals.

-**Samuel Adams** Founding Father, Leader of the Sons of Liberty[76]

Virtue or morality is a necessary spring of popular government. The rule indeed extends with more or less force to every species of free government ... Promote, then, as an object of primary importance, institutions for the general diffusion of knowledge. In proportion as the structure of a government gives force to public opinion, it is essential that public opinion should be enlightened.

- **President George Washington** First President of the United States of America Farewell Address, 1796[77]

CHAPTER TWELVE

RELIABLE RESOURCES

Below are some resources to help you get started in becoming informed, engaged, and involved. I've included a short description of each resource to help you know a little more about what they provide.

1. **The Barna Group** - https://www.barna.com/
   A good source of data, data analysis, national surveys, and Biblical analysis of the current state of the culture.

2. **The Heritage Foundation** - https://www.heritage.org/
   A watchdog group on Capitol Hill, providing the latest updates and information on legislative actions under consideration by the federal government. Membership is affordable and subscriptions to email updates are free.

3. **The Daily Signal** - www.thedailysignal.com
   A great source for news on a variety of issues. A branch of the Heritage Foundation.

4. **The American Institute for Economic Research** - https://www.aier.org/
   Follow them on social media such as LinkedIn to read the latest articles, data, and analysis regarding economic and free market issues.

5. **Alliance Defending Freedom** - https://adflegal.org/
   A legal group of Christian lawyers, working to defend the rights of all Americans which are guaranteed in

the Bill of Rights. They have defended and won free speech, religious freedom, and other major cases at the US Supreme Court. They have regional directors who will come to your church, present their mission, and allow your church to become a member in order to safeguard your rights against government intrusion and persecution.

6. **Family Research Council** - https://www.frc.org/
Supporting traditional family values on Capitol Hill and in every state, FRC and FRCAction have been a reliable source for information on issues and a Biblical worldview on current issues.

7. **Live Action - Pro-Life Organization** - https://www.liveaction.org/
Investigating the abortion industry and exposing the corruption. They provide excellent, up-to-date informative videos for young people regarding the issue of pre-born life.

8. **The Radiance Foundation** - https://radiancefoundation.org/
Unique presentations, taking on the controversial issues of the day and speaking Biblical truth in powerful ways to the next generation.

9. **Susan B. Anthony Pro-Life America** - https://sbaprolife.org
Longtime pro-life group, lobbying Congress and now organizing grassroots activists by endorsing pro-life candidates and working to elect strong, pro-life leaders on every level.

10. **Ballotopia** - https://ballotpedia.org/Main_Page
A good resource for learning what will be on the ballot and even how certain elected officials have voted in the past.

11. **Media Research Center** - https://www.mrc.org/
Exposing bias in the media by documenting the content presented by mainstream media across the country. They have been a stalwart of truth in the world of media for many years.

12. **Wall Builders** - https://www.wallbuilders.com
Excellent source for learning all about America's Christian history. They have a huge library of original documents and give amazing tours of Capitol Hill.

13. **Patriot Academy** - https://www.patriotacademy.com/
A great educational experience for young people in junior high and high school to learn the legislative process, the debate process, and how to stand strong for Christian values.

14. **The Washington Times** - www.washingtontimes.com
A conservative news outlet, worth the subscription.

15. **The Epoch Times** - https://www.theepochtimes.com
Another good resource for news from a conservative view.

16. **Foundation for Economic Education** - www.fee.org
Excellent articles, lectures, and information on the free market system and how it affects every day Americans.

17. **Tracking US Senate Votes** - https://www.senate.gov/legislative/votes_new.htm

18. **Politico - Political News** - www.politico.com
Focused on politics in Washington, DC – leans liberal.

19. **US House & Senate Roll Call Votes** - https://www.congress.gov/roll-call-votes

20. **GovTrack** - US Congress Vote Tracking - https://www.govtrack.us/congress/votes

21. **Vote View** - Research political trends and vote records - https://voteview.com/

22. **Pew Research (data)** - www.pewresearch.org
Great data and research on a variety of subjects.

23. **The Washington, Jefferson & Madison Institute** -
http://www.wjmi.org/

24. **The March for Life** - www.marchforlife.org
Marching in Washington for Life since 1974, worth the
trip and research into your state March for Life.

25. **Focus on the Family** - www.focusonthefamily.com
Longstanding resource for Biblical training and information for the family.

26. **Concerned Women of America** – https://concerned-
women.org
A conservative national organization for women who
want to be involved in the political process.

27. **Salt and Light Council** - www.saltandlightcouncil.org
- Educational seminars and resources for the church to
be active in government.

EXCERPTS FROM THE REPUBLICAN PLATFORM -2023

https://prod-cdn-static.gop.com/static/home/data/platform.pdf
www.gopconvention2016.com

2020 RESOLUTIONS AND THE REPUBLICAN PARTY PLATFORM

WHEREAS, The Republican National Committee (RNC) has significantly scaled back the size and scope of the 2020 Republican National Convention in Charlotte due to strict restrictions on gatherings and meetings, and out of concern for the safety of convention attendees and our hosts;

WHEREAS, The RNC has unanimously voted to forego the Convention Committee on Platform, in appreciation of the fact that it did not want a small contingent of delegates formulating a new platform without the breadth of perspectives within the ever-growing Republican movement;

RESOLVED, That the 2020 Republican National Convention will adjourn without adopting a new platform until the 2024 Republican National Convention;

Marriage, Family, and Society

Foremost among those institutions is the American family. It is the foundation of civil society, and the cornerstone of the family is natural marriage, the union of one man and one woman...

Strong families, depending upon God and one another, advance the cause of liberty by lessening the need for government in their daily lives. Conversely, as we have learned over the last five decades, the loss of faith and family life leads to greater dependence upon government. That is why Republicans formulate public policy, from taxation to education, from healthcare to welfare, with attention to the needs and strengths of the family...

Moreover, marriage remains the greatest antidote to child poverty... The reality remains that millions of American families do not have the advantages that come with that structure. We honor the courageous efforts of those who bear the burdens of parenting alone and embrace the principle that all Americans should be treated with dignity and respect. But respect is not enough.

Our laws and our government's regulations should recognize marriage as the union of one man and one woman and actively promote married family life as

... the basis of a stable and prosperous society. For that reason ... we do not accept the Supreme Court's redefinition of marriage and we urge its reversal, whether through judicial reconsideration or a constitutional amendment returning control over marriage to the states.

We urge marriage penalties to be removed from the tax code and public assistance programs.

We oppose government discrimination against businesses or entities which decline to sell items or services to individuals for activities that go against their religious views about such activities. To protect religious liberty we will ensure that faith-based institutions, especially those that are vital parts of underserved neighborhoods, do not face discrimination by government.

A Culture of Hope

Republicans propose to evaluate a poverty program by whether it actually reduces poverty and increases the personal independence of its participants ... Intergenerational poverty has persisted and worsened since 1966.

...It has been 20 years since the landmark Republican welfare reform of 1996 broke away from the discredited Great Society model. By making welfare a benefit instead of an entitlement, it put millions of recipients on a transition from dependence to independence. Welfare rolls declined by half ... Best of all, about 3 million children moved out of poverty. Today that progress has been lost.

This is the progressive pathology: Keeping people dependent so that government can redistribute income. The result is 45.8 million people on food stamps and 77 million on Medicaid, plus another 5.7 million in the Children's Health Insurance Program. This is the false compassion of the status quo.

We propose instead the dynamic compassion of work requirements in a growing economy, where opportunity takes the place of a hand-out, where true self-esteem can grow from the satisfaction of a job well done.

We call for removal of structural impediments: Over-regulation of start-up enterprises, excessive licensing requirements, needless restrictions on formation of schools and day-care centers serving neighborhood families, and restrictions on providing public services in fields like transport and sanitation that close the opportunity door to all but a favored few.

We will continue our fight for school choice until all parents can find good, safe schools for their children.

Title IX

We emphatically support the original, authentic meaning of Title IX ... of 1972. It affirmed that "no person in the United States shall, on the basis of sex, be excluded from participation in, be denied the benefits of, or be subjected to discrimination under any education program or activity receiving Federal financial assistance." … That same provision of law is now being used … to impose a social and cultural revolution upon the American people by wrongly redefining sex discrimination to include sexual orientation or other categories. Their agenda has nothing to do with individual rights; it has everything to do with power. They are determined to reshape our schools — and our entire society — to fit the mold of an ideology alien to America's history and traditions.

Their edict to the states concerning restrooms, locker rooms, and other facilities is at once illegal, dangerous, and ignores privacy issues. We salute the several states which have filed suit against it.

The … distortion of Title IX to micromanage the way colleges and universities deal with allegations of abuse contravenes our country's legal traditions and must be halted before it further muddles this complex issue and prevents the proper authorities from investigating and prosecuting sexual assault effectively with due process.

Education: A Chance for Every Child

Education is much more than schooling … It is the handing over of a cultural identity. That is why American education has … been the focus of constant controversy, as centralizing forces from outside the family and community have sought to remake education in order to remake America. They have done immense damage.

The federal government should not be a partner in that effort, as the Constitution gives it no role in education. Parents are a child's first and foremost

… educators, and have primary responsibility for the education of their children. Parents have a right to direct their children's education, care, and upbringing.

We support a constitutional amendment to protect that right from interference by states, the federal government, or international bodies such as the United Nations. We reject a one- size-fits-all approach to education and support a broad range of choices for parents and children at the state and local level.

We oppose … the imposition of national standards and assessments, encourage the parents and educators who are implementing alternatives to Common Core, and congratulate the states which have successfully repealed it. Their education reform movement calls for choice-based, parent-driven accountability at every stage of schooling … It recognizes the wisdom of local control of our schools…

We applaud America's great teachers, who should be protected against frivolous lawsuits and should be able to take reasonable actions to maintain discipline and order in the classroom.

A good understanding of the Bible being indispensable for the development of an educated citizenry, we encourage state legislatures to offer the Bible in a literature curriculum as an elective in American high schools. …

Rigid tenure systems should be replaced with a merit-based approach in order to attract the best talent to the classroom. All personnel who interact with school children should pass background checks and be held to the highest standards of personal conduct.

We support options for learning, including home-schooling, career and technical education, private or parochial schools, magnet schools, charter schools, online learning, and early-college high schools. We especially support the innovative financing mechanisms that make options available to all children: education savings accounts (ESAs), vouchers, and tuition tax credits.

We propose that the bulk of federal money through Title I for low-income children and through IDEA for children with special needs should follow the child to whatever school the family thinks will work best for them.

We renew our call for replacing "family planning" programs for teens with sexual risk avoidance education that sets abstinence until marriage as the responsible and respected standard of behavior. That approach — the only one always effective against premarital pregnancy and sexually-transmitted disease — empowers teens to achieve optimal health outcomes.

We oppose school-based clinics that provide referral or counseling for abortion and contraception and believe that federal funds should not be used in mandatory or universal mental health, psychiatric, or socio-emotional screening programs.

Restoring Patient Control and Preserving Quality in Healthcare

We must recover the traditional patient-physician relationship based on mutual trust, informed consent, and confidentiality. To simplify the system for both patients and providers, we will reduce mandates and enable insurers and providers of care to increase healthcare options and contain costs.

We will return to the states their historic role of regulating local insurance markets, limit federal requirements on both private insurance and Medicaid, and call on state officials to reconsider the costly medical mandates, imposed under their own laws, that price millions of low-income families out of the insurance market.

To guarantee first-rate care for the needy, we propose to block grant Medicaid and other payments and to assist all patients, including those with pre-existing conditions, to obtain coverage in a robust consumer market.

We ... affirm the dignity of women by protecting the sanctity of human life. Numerous studies have shown that abortion endangers the health and well- being of women, and we stand firmly against it.

We will promote price transparency so consumers can know the cost of treatments before they agree to them. We will empower individuals and small businesses to form purchasing pools in order to expand coverage to the uninsured.

We believe that individuals with preexisting conditions who maintain continuous coverage should be protected from discrimination. We applaud the

Restoring Patient Control and Preserving Quality in Healthcare

... advance of technology in electronic medical records while affirming patient privacy and ownership of personal health information.

Consumer choice is the most powerful factor in healthcare reform. The need to maintain coverage should not dictate where families have to live and work. We propose to end tax discrimination against the individual purchase of insurance and allow consumers to buy insurance across state lines.

We look to the growth of Health Savings Accounts and Health Reimbursement Accounts that empower patients and advance choice in healthcare.

Our aging population must have access to safe and affordable care. Because most seniors desire to age at home, we will make homecare a priority in public policy and will implement programs to protect against elder abuse.

Protecting Individual Conscience in Healthcare

We respect the rights of conscience of healthcare professionals, doctors, nurses, pharmacists, and organizations, especially the faith-based groups which provide a major portion of care for the nation and the needy.

We support the ability of all organizations to provide, purchase, or enroll in healthcare coverage consistent with their religious, moral, or ethical convictions without discrimination or penalty.

We support the right of parents to determine the proper medical treatment and therapy for their minor children. We support the right of parents to consent to medical treatment for their minor children and urge enactment of legislation that would require parental consent for their daughter to be transported across state lines for abortion.

American taxpayers should not be forced to fund abortion. We call for a permanent ban on federal funding and subsidies for abortion and healthcare plans that include abortion coverage.

Better Care and Lower Costs: Tort Reform

We support state and federal legislation to cap non-economic damages in medical malpractice lawsuits, thereby relieving conscientious providers of burdens that are not rightly theirs and addressing a serious cause of higher medical bills.

Advancing Research and Development in Healthcare

We call for expanded support for the stem cell research that now offers the greatest hope for many afflictions — through adult stem cells, umbilical cord blood, and cells reprogrammed into pluripotent stem cells — without the destruction of embryonic human life.

We urge a ban on human cloning for research or reproduction, and a ban on the creation of, or experimentation on, human embryos for research.

We believe the FDA's approval of Mifeprex, a dangerous abortifacient formerly known as RU-486, threatens women's health, as does the agency's endorsement of over-the-counter sales of powerful contraceptives without a physician's recommendation.

National Defense

The Republican Party is the party of peace through strength. We believe that American exceptionalism— the notion that our ideas and principles as a nation give us a unique place of moral leadership in the world — requires the United States to retake its natural position as leader of the free world. Tyranny and injustice thrive when America is weakened. The oppressed have no greater ally than a confident and determined United States, backed by the strongest military on the planet.

Quite simply, the Republican Party is committed to rebuilding the U.S. military into the strongest on earth, with vast superiority over any other nation or group of nations in the world. We face a dangerous world, and we believe in a resurgent America.

We support the rights of conscience of military chaplains of all faiths to practice their faith free from political interference. We reject attempts … to censure and silence them, particularly Christians and Christian chaplains.

We support an increase in the size of the Chaplain Corps … will protect the religious freedom of all military members, especially chaplains, and will not tolerate attempts to ban Bibles or religious symbols from military facilities.

We will also encourage education regarding the religious liberties of military personnel under both the First Amendment of the U.S. Constitution and the current National Defense Authorization Act.

EXCERPTS FROM THE DEMOCRAT PLATFORM -2023

https://democrats.org/where-we-stand/party-platform/
The Democrat Party Platform

Supporting Faith and Service

Religious freedom is a core American value and a core value of the Democratic Party. Democrats will protect the rights of each

American for the free exercise of his or her own religion. It will be the policy of the Democratic Administration to advocate for religious freedom throughout the world.

Democrats celebrate America's history of religious pluralism and tolerance, and recognize the countless acts of service of our faith communities, as well as the paramount importance of maintaining the separation between church and state enshrined in our Constitution.

... Too many of our religious communities have been victimized by acts of intolerance, bigotry, and violence. Democrats will increase funding and support for security investments and protection at houses of worship, because everyone should be able to pray without fear.

We will confront white nationalist terrorism and combat hate crimes perpetrated against religious minorities.

Democrats also recognize that, to fully confront the legacy of systemic and structural racism, it is time to examine, confront and dismantle the government programs, policies and practices that have unfairly targeted American Muslims as security threats. We condemn the decades-long campaign to demonize and dehumanize the Muslim faith community, which has led to increased rates of violence and discrimination targeting American Muslims or those perceived to be Muslim.

We will hold accountable those who engage in or enable violent or other illegal activity targeting religious minorities, including by directing the federal government to address the growing and violent threat of white supremacist, neo-Nazi and anti-government groups.

REFORMING OUR CRIMINAL JUSTICE SYSTEM

Democrats believe we need to overhaul the criminal justice system from top to bottom. Police brutality is a stain on the soul of our nation. It is unacceptable that millions of people in our country have good reason to fear they may lose their lives in a routine traffic stop, or while standing on a street corner, or while playing with a toy in a public park.

Democrats also recognize that all too often, systematic cuts to public services have left police officers on the front lines of responding to social challenges for which they have not been trained, from homelessness to mental health crises to the opioid epidemic. We can and must do better for our communities.

This is the moment to root out structural and systemic racism in our criminal justice system and our society, and reimagine public safety for the benefit of our people and the character of our country.

We must start by preventing people from entering the criminal justice system in the first place. Democrats believe we must break the school-to-prison pipeline that too often relies on arrests and law enforcement to address misbehavior that ought to be handled and deescalated within the school.

We support re-issuing federal guidance from the Department of Education and the Department of Justice to prevent the disparate disciplinary treatment of children of color and children with disabilities in school and educational settings.

Democrats believe every school should have sufficient funding to employ guidance counselors, social workers, nurses, or school psychologists to help guarantee age-appropriate and racially equitable student disciplinary practices, rather than turning to police to resolve these issues.

Democrats believe we must ensure real accountability for individual and systemic misconduct in our police departments, prevent law enforcement from becoming unnecessarily entangled in the everyday lives of Americans, and reimagine policing for the benefit and safety of the American people.

In recent years, some innovative police departments have enacted evidence-based reforms to change their approach by investing in robust training and putting in place—and, even more crucially, enforcing—strong standards governing   conflict resolution, de-es-calation, and use of force. We must build on these evidence-based approaches and implement them nationwide.

Democrats will establish strict national standards governing the use of force, including banning the use of chokeholds and ca-rotid holds and permitting deadly force only when necessary and a last resort to prevent an imminent threat to life. Americans must feel safe when they are asleep in their own homes.

We will require immediate application of these standards to all federal law enforcement agencies and condition federal grants on their adoption at the state and local level.

We will require officer training in effective nonviolent tactics, appropriate use of force, implicit bias, and peer intervention, both at the academy and on the job. And we will ban racial and religious profiling in law enforcement.

Democrats will support measures to improve training and ed-ucation for judges, corrections officers, prosecutors, public defend-ers, and police officers to ensure transgender and gender non-con-forming people receive fair and equitable treatment in the criminal justice system.

Protecting Women's Rights

Democrats will fight to guarantee equal rights for women, including by ratifying the Equal Rights Amendment and at long last enshrining gender equality in the U.S. Constitution.

We will take aggressive action to end pay inequality, including by increasing penalties against companies that discriminate against women and passing the Paycheck Fairness Act.

Democrats are committed to ending sexual assault, domestic abuse, and other violence against women, including the epidemics of violence against Native American women and transgender wom-en of color.

Democrats believe every woman should be able to access high-quality reproductive health care services, including safe and legal abortion.

We oppose and will fight to overturn federal and state laws that create barriers to women's reproductive health and rights, including by repealing the Hyde Amendment and protecting and codifying the right to reproductive freedom.

Democrats will take action to protect the rights of pregnant women in the workplace, including by requiring employers to make reasonable accommodations for pregnant and breastfeeding workers and those who have recently given birth and at last joining other advanced economies by enacting paid sick days and universal paid family and medical leave.

Protecting LGBTQ+ Rights

Democrats applaud [the 2020] U.S. Supreme Court decision that made clear that employment discrimination based on sexual orientation and gender identity violates the law, but we know we still have work to do to ensure LGBTQ+ people are treated equally under the law and in our society.

We will fight to enact the Equality Act and at last outlaw discrimination against LGBTQ+ people in housing, public accommodations, access to credit, education, jury service, and federal programs.

We will work to ensure LGBTQ+ people are not discriminated against when seeking to adopt or foster children, protect LGBTQ+ children from bullying and assault, and guarantee transgender students' access to facilities based on their gender identity.

Democrats will ensure federally funded programs for older adults are inclusive for LGBTQ+ seniors.

Recognizing that LGBTQ+ youth and adults suffer from significant health disparities, including mental health and substance use disorders, Democrats will expand mental health and suicide prevention services, and ban harmful "conversion therapy" practices.

We will ensure that all transgender and non-binary people can procure official government identification documents that accurately reflect their gender identity.

We will stop employment discrimination in the federal government, and will restore full implementation of President Obama's executive order prohibiting discrimination by federal contractors on the basis of sexual orientation and gender identity.

ACHIEVING UNIVERSAL, AFFORDABLE, QUALITY HEALTH CARE

We are proud to be the party of Medicare, Medicaid, and the Affordable Care Act. Because of the Obama-Biden Administration and the Affordable Care Act, more than 100 million Americans with pre-existing conditions, from heart disease to asthma, are secure in the knowledge that insurance companies can no longer discriminate against them. And more Americans are able to get health coverage than ever before.

Democrats will keep up the fight until all Americans can access secure, affordable, high-quality health insurance—because as Democrats, we fundamentally believe health care is a right for all, not a privilege for the few.

The burdens of this pandemic have not been borne equally, as communities of color have suffered higher rates of infection and death, and struggled to access life-saving care when they need it most. Our essential workers have been deemed expendable...

Democrats believe we need to protect, strengthen, and build upon our bedrock health care programs, including the Affordable Care Act, Medicare, Medicaid, and the Veterans Affairs (VA) system. Private insurers need real competition to ensure they have incentive to provide affordable, quality coverage to every American.

We will give all Americans the choice to select a high-quality, affordable public option through the Affordable Care Act marketplace. The public option will provide at least one plan choice without deductibles; will be administered by CMS, not private companies; and will cover all primary care without any co-payments and control costs for other treatments by negotiating prices with doctors and hospitals, just like Medicare does on behalf of older people.

The lowest-income Americans, including more than four million adults who should be eligible for Medicaid but who live in states where Republican governors have refused to expand the program, will be automatically enrolled in the public option without premiums; they may opt out at any time.

We will enable millions of older workers to choose between their employer-provided plans, the public option, or enrolling in Medicare when they turn 60, instead of having to wait until they are 65.

Democrats are categorically opposed to raising the Medicare retirement age.

The opioid epidemic has devastated American communities. Democrats will make medication-assisted treatment available to all who need it, and will require publicly supported health clinics to offer medication-assisted treatment for opioid addiction and approved treatments for other substance use disorders.

We believe we must stop over-prescribing while improving access to effective and needed pain management.

Democrats recognize that incarcerated people suffer from serious mental health and substance use disorders at higher rates than the general population, which is why we will support expanded access to mental health and substance use disorder care in prisons and for returning citizens.

We will ensure no one is incarcerated solely for drug use, and support increased use of drug courts, harm reduction interventions, and treatment diversion programs for those struggling with substance use disorders.

Democrats will launch a sustained, government-wide effort …
to eliminate racial, ethnic, gender, and geographic gaps in insurance
rates, access to quality care, and health outcomes. That includes
tackling the social, economic, and environmental inequities—the
social determinants of health like poor housing, hunger, inade-
quate transportation, mass incarceration, air and water pollution,
and gun violence—that contribute to worse health outcomes for
low-income Americans and people of color. We can and must fix
these inequities by expanding coverage, making health care more
affordable, and tackling implicit bias in our health care system.

Democrats will ensure that people with disabilities are never denied coverage based on the use of quality-adjusted life year
(QALY) indexes.

Democrats will ensure federal data collection and analysis is
adequately funded and designed to allow for disaggregation by
race, gender, sexual orientation, gender identity, geography, dis-
ability status, national origin, and other important variables, so that
disparities in health coverage, access, and outcomes can be better
understood and addressed.

We will expand access to health care for people living and
working across the United States by extending Affordable Care Act
coverage to Dreamers, and working with Congress to lift the five-
year waiting period for Medicaid and Children's Health Insurance
Program eligibility for low-income, lawfully present immigrants.

Democrats remain committed to ending the HIV/AIDS epidemic, which disproportionately affects communities of color and
the LGBTQ+ community, and will support critical investments under the Ryan White HIV/AIDS Program and the Minority HIV/
AIDS Fund.

COMBATING THE CLIMATE CRISIS AND PURSUING ENVIRONMENTAL JUSTICE

Climate change is a global emergency. We have no time to waste in taking action to protect Americans' lives and futures. Like so many crises facing the United States, the impacts of climate change are not evenly distributed in our society or our economy. Communities of color, low-income families, and Indigenous communities have long suffered disproportionate and cumulative harm from air pollution, water pollution, and toxic sites.

Although the youngest generations of Americans have contributed the least to this calamity, they stand to lose the most as they suffer from the impacts of runaway carbon pollution for decades to come.

We can and must build a thriving, equitable, and globally competitive clean energy economy that puts workers and communities first and leaves no one behind. We will help rebuild our economy from the COVID-19 pandemic...by mobilizing historic, transformative public and private investments to launch a clean energy revolution.

We believe the scientists: the window for unprecedented and necessary action is closing, and closing fast. We will use federal resources and authorities across all agencies to deploy proven clean energy solutions; create millions of family-supporting and union jobs; upgrade and make resilient our energy, water, wastewater, and transportation infrastructure; and develop and manufacture next-generation technologies to address the climate crisis right here in the United States.

We will do all this with an eye to equity, access, benefits, and ownership opportunities for frontline communities—because Democrats believe we must embed environmental justice, economic justice, and climate justice at the heart of our policy and governing agenda.

We will rejoin the Paris Climate Agreement and, on day one, seek higher ambition from nations around the world, putting the United States back in the position of global leadership where we belong.

We will follow science and the law by reducing harmful methane and carbon pollution from the energy sector.

Democrats will make investments to create millions of family-supporting and union jobs in clean energy generation, energy efficiency, clean transportation, advanced manufacturing, and sustainable agriculture across America.

All jobs in the clean energy economy should provide an opportunity to join a union. Democrats will restore and protect workers' rights to organize and bargain collectively.

We will invest in the education and training of underrepresented groups, including people of color, low-income Americans, women, veterans, people with disabilities, and unemployed energy workers for jobs in clean energy-related industries, especially union jobs that provide strong opportunities for economic advancement.

Democrats will also mobilize a diverse new generation of young workers through a corps and cohort challenged to conserve our public lands; deliver new clean energy, including to low-income communities and communities of color; and address the changing climate, including through pre-apprenticeship opportunities, joint labor-management registered apprenticeships for training, and direct-hire programs that put good-paying and union jobs within reach for more Americans.

We agree with scientists and public health experts that the United States—and the world—must achieve net-zero greenhouse gas emissions as soon as possible, and no later than 2050.

In the interest of time, I will not include any other national party platforms, but I have included links to them below.

LIBERTARIAN NATIONAL PARTY

https://www.lp.org/platform/

THE GREEN PARTY OF THE UNITED STATES

https://www.gp.org/platform

END NOTES

1. *KJV, Reference Bible: Holy Bible, King James Version.* Nashville: Thomas Nelson, 2005. Psalm 77:5, 7, 10-11, 14.
2. "Declaration of Independence: A Transcription." National Archives. Last modified June 8, 2022. https://www.archives.gov/founding-docs/declaration-transcript.
3. "The U.S. Constitution: Preamble." United States Courts. Accessed April 30, 2023. https://www.uscourts.gov/about-federal-courts/educational-resources/about-educational-outreach/activity-resources/us.
4. Tyler Page, William. "The American's Creed." US History. Accessed April 30, 2023. https://www.ushistory.org/documents/creed.htm.
5. Bradford, William. "Of Plymouth Plantation: Bradford's History of the Plymouth Settlement, 1608-1650." *San Antonio, TX: Vision Forum*, 1998, 21.
6. Carver, John et. al. "The Mayflower Compact." General Society of Mayflower Descendants. Accessed May 3, 2023. https://the-mayflowersociety.org/history/the-mayflower-compact/.
7. Bradford, William, "Of Plymouth Plantation."
8. Winthrop, John. "A Model of Christian Charity." Teaching American History. Last modified July 8, 2022. https://teachingamericanhistory.org/document/a-model-of-christian-charity-2/.
9. Winthrop, John et. al. "The Articles of Confederation of the United Colonies of New England; May 19, 1643." Avalon Project - Documents in Law, History and Diplomacy. Accessed July 3, 2023.

https://avalon.law.yale.edu/17th_century/art1613.asp.
10. DeMar, Gary. *America's Christian Heritage.* Nashville, TN: B&H Books, 2003.
11. Hall, Mark D. "Did America Have a Christian Founding?" The Heritage Foundation. Accessed July 3, 2023. https://www.heritage.org/political-process/report/did-america-have-christian-founding#.
12. Carver, John et. al. "The Mayflower Compact."
13. Bradford, William. *Of Plymouth Plantation.* New York: Samuel Eliot Morrison, Alfred Knopf, 1952. 9.
14. Thorpe, Francis N. *The Federal and State Constitutions, Colonial Charters, and Other Organic Laws of the State, Territories, and Colonies Now Or Heretofore Forming the United States of America.* Washington, DC: Government Printing Office, 1909.
15. Wirt, William. *Sketches of the Life and Character of Patrick Henry.* Philadelphia/New York: Lewis Copeland & Lawrence. W. Lamm, 1973. As reproduced in The World's Greatest Speeches.
16. Dreisbach, Daniel L., and Mark D. Hall. *The Sacred Rights of Conscience: Selected Readings on Religious Liberty and Church-state Relations in the American Founding.* Carmel, IN: Liberty Fund, 2009. 236-238, 441-475.
17. Washington, George. "Founders Online: General Orders, 4 July 1775." Founders Online. Accessed May 7, 2023. https://founders.archives.gov/documents/Washington/03-01-02-0027.
18. Marshall, Peter J., and David B. Manuel. *The Light and the Glory (God's Plan for America Book #1).* Old Tappan, NJ: Revell, 1977. 365.
19. Gordon, William. "A Sermon Preached Before the Honorable House of Representatives, on the Day Intended for the Choice of Counsellors, Agreeable to the Advice of the Continental Congress. / By William Gordon, Pastor of the Third Church in Roxbury." U-M Library Digital Collections. n.d. https://quod.lib.umich.edu/e/evans/N11106.0001.001/1:4?rgn=div1;view=fulltext.

20. Muhlenberg, Henry A. *The Life of Major-General Peter Muhlenberg: Of the Revolutionary Army*. Phiadelphia, PA: Carey & Hart, 1849. 52-54.

21. "Rev. James Caldwell." Website. Accessed May 7, 2023. https://www.unionnjhistory.com/james-and-hannah-caldwell.

22. Americanwarsus. "Battle of Springfield." American Revolutionary War. Last modified January 15, 2018. https://revolutionary-war.us/year-1780/battle-of-springfield/.

23. Burk, W.Herbert. *Washington's Prayers*. 1907. 87.

24. Hall, Mark D. "Did America Have a Christian Founding?" The Heritage Foundation. n.d. https://www.heritage.org/political-process/report/did-america-have-christian-founding#.

25. "Declaration of Independence: A Transcription." National Archives. Last modified June 8, 2022. https://www.archives.gov/founding-docs/declaration-transcript.

26. Soodalter, Ron. "How George Washington's Thanksgiving Proclamation Caused a Ruckus in Congress." HistoryNet. Last modified November 16, 2022. https://www.historynet.com/washingtons-first-thanksgiving/.

27. United States Congress. Documentary History of the First Federal Congress of the United States of America, March 4, 1789-March 3, 1791: Petition Histories and Non-Legislative Official Documents. Johns Hopkins University Press, 1974. vol. 11.

28. Dreisbach, Daniel L., and Mark D. Hall. *The Sacred Rights of Conscience: Selected Readings on Religious Liberty and Church-state Relations in the American Founding*. Carmel, IN: Liberty Fund, 2009. 236-238, 441-475.

29. Hall, Mark D. "Did America Have a Christian Founding?" The Heritage Foundation. n.d. https://www.heritage.org/political-process/report/did-america-have-christian-founding#.

30. Adams, John. "Founders Online: From John Adams to James Warren, 22 April 1776." Founders Online. Accessed April 30, 2023. https://founders.archives.gov/documents/Ad-

ams/06-04-02-0052.

31. McHenry, James. *Papers of Dr. James McHenry on the Federal Convention of 1787.* The American Historical Review of the Library of Congress Manuscript Division, doi: 10.1086/ahr/11.3.595, 1906.

32. Adams, John. "Founders Online: From John Adams to James Warren, 22 April 1776." Founders Online. Accessed April 30, 2023. https://founders.archives.gov/documents/Adams/06-04-02-0052.

33. Liberty Fund, ed. "The Correspondence and Public Papers of John Jay, Vol. 4 (1794-1826)." Online Library of Liberty. n.d. https://oll.libertyfund.org/title/johnston-the-correspondence-and-public-papers-of-john-jay-vol-4-1794-1826.

34. Paine, Thomas. *The Writings of Thomas Paine*, 1st ed. New York, NY: Putnam's Sons, 1894. 2.

35. Mosley, Patrina, and David Closson. "For Christians, Voting Is Not an Option. It Is a Divine Calling." FRC. Accessed May 7, 2023. https://www.frc.org/get.cfm?i=PV18K12.

36. Runes, Dagobert D. *The Selected Writings of Benjamin Rush - Primary Source Edition.* New York, NY: Nabu Press, 1947.

37. Adams, John. "Founders Online: From John Adams to James Warren, 22 April 1776." Founders Online. Accessed April 30, 2023. https://founders.archives.gov/documents/Adams/06-04-02-0052.

38. Garfield, James A. "A Century of Congress." The Atlantic Monthly. April, 1877.

39. United States Senate Historical Office. "Washington's Farewell Address to the People of the United States." GovInfo | U.S. Government Publishing Office. n.d. https://www.govinfo.gov/content/pkg/GPO-CDOC-106sdoc21/pdf/GPO-CDOC-106sdoc21.pdf.

40. Acton, Lord. "The History of Freedom in Antiquity." Acton Institute. Last modified January 20, 2023. https://www.acton.org/research/history-freedom-antiquity.

41. Barna, George. *The Seven Faith Tribes: Who They Are, What They Believe, and Why They Matter.* Ventura, CA: BarnaBooks, 2011.

42. Barna, George. "America's Seven Faith Tribes Hold the Key to National Restoration." Barna Group. Accessed April 30, 2023. https://www.barna.com/research/americas-seven-faith-tribes-hold-the-key-to-national-restoration/.

43. Webster, Noah. History of the United States. New Haven, CT. Durrie & Peck. 336, 337. Instructive and Entertaining Lessons for Youth; With Rules for Reading with Propriety, Illustrated by Examples: Designed for Use in Schools and Families. New Haven, CT. S.Babcock and Durrie & Peck.

44. Barna Group. "Porn in the Digital Age: New Research Reveals 10 Trends." Barna Group. n.d. https://www.barna.com/research/porn-in-the-digital-age-new-research-reveals-10-trends/.

45. Hegseth, Pete, and David Goodwin. *Battle for the American Mind: Uprooting a Century of Miseducation.* New York: HarperCollins, 2022. 50, 51.

46. The Correspondence and Public Papers of John Jay, vol. 4. (1794-1826) New York/London. G.P. Putnam's Sons Letter to Representative John Murray, October 12, 1816.

47. Stevenson II, Adlai. "The Nature of Patriotism." Adlai Today. n.d. https://adlaitoday.org/articles/think3_patriotism_08-27-52.pdf. Address the American Legion Convention, Madison Square Garden, New York City.

48. Scalia, Justice Antonin. "Opening Testimony October 5, 2011." C-SPAN.org. n.d. https://www.c-span.org/video/?c4478650/user-clip-justice-scalia-gridlock.

49. Warner Brothers. "Who Do You Think You Are? Valerie Bertinelli." TLC. n.d. https://go.tlc.com/video/who-do-you-think-you-are-tlc-atve-us/valerie-bertinelli.

50. Stutzman, Christy. "America's National Identity Crisis: Solved." The Washington Times. Last modified September 5, 2014. https://www.washingtontimes.com/news/2014/sep/5/

stutzman-americas-national-identity-crisis-solved/?utm_campaign=shareaholic&utm_medium=copy_link&utm_source=bookmark.

51. Streets, Priscilla W. Lewis Walker of Chester Valley and His Descendants: With Some of the Families with Whom They Are Connected by Marriage, 1686-1896. London, UK. Forgotten Books, 2016.

52. Trueman, Carl R. The Rise and Triumph of the Modern Self: Cultural Amnesia, Expressive Individualism, and the Road to Sexual Revolution. Wheaton, IL. Crossway, 2020. 226, 228.

53. Trueman. Modern Self. 250.

54. Cicero, Marcus T. *Cicero De Re Publica: Selections.* Cambridge, UK: Cambridge University Press, 1995. LCL213:210-211.

55. Gramsci, Antonio. "Selections from the Prison Notebooks of Antonio Gramsci." *Oxford Bibliographies.* n.d. https://www.oxford-bibliographies.com/display/document/obo-9780190221911/obo-9780190221911-0043.xml.

56. Trueman. Modern Self. 259.

57. Barna Group. "Changes in Worldview Among Christians over the Past 13 Years." Barna Group. n.d. https://www.barna.com/research/barna-survey-examines-changes-in-worldview-among-christians-over-the-past-13-years/.

58. Mitchell, Travis. "In U.S., Decline of Christianity Continues at Rapid Pace." Pew Research Center's Religion & Public Life Project. Last modified June 9, 2020. https://www.pewresearch.org/religion/2019/10/17/in-u-s-decline-of-christianity-continues-at-rapid-pace/.

59. Josephson, Kimberlee. "The Rise of ESG, Replacing Profits with Paternalism, and Strategy with Standards." AIER. Last modified August 28, 2022. https://www.aier.org/article/the-rise-of-esg-replacing-profits-with-paternalism-and-strategy-with-standards/.

60. Wolf, Brett. "ESG Gap Widens: EU Rules Become More Prescriptive As US Proposals Wait in the Wings." Thomson Reu-

ters Institute. Last modified June 1, 2022. https://www.thomsonreuters.com/en-us/posts/investigation-fraud-and-risk/esg-gap-widens/.

61. Yongguan, Pan. "CHINA PASTOR: "This Could Be Our Last Sunday Together."" VOM Radio. n.d. https://www.vomradio.net/episodes/detail/china-pastor-this-could-be-our-last-sunday-together?_source_code=EM23D4.

62. Moore, Mark, and Mark Lungariello. "North Korean Defector Slams 'woke' US Schools." New York Post. Last modified June 15, 2021. https://nypost.com/2021/06/14/north-korean-defector-slams-woke-us-schools/.

63. Park, Yeonmi, and Maryanne Vollers. *In Order to Live: A North Korean Girl's Journey to Freedom.* London: Penguin, 2016.

64. Shakespeare, William. "Macbeth and Hecate." Shakespeare Online. n.d. https://www.shakespeare-online.com/faq/macbeth-faq/hecate.html.

65. Mill, John S. *Inaugural Address: Delivered to the University of St. Andrews, Feb. 1st, 1867.* London: Longmas, Green, Reader, and Dyer, 1867.

66. Hegseth and Goodwin, Battle for the American Mind. 47-48, 99.

67. Pew Research Center. "Russians Return to Religion, But Not to Church." Pew Research Center's Religion & Public Life Project. Last modified May 31, 2020. https://www.pewresearch.org/religion/2014/02/10/russians-return-to-religion-but-not-to-church/.

68. Reich, Wilhelm. The Mass Psychology of Fascism. London: Macmillan, 1970. 30.

69. Trueman. Modern Self. 235.

70. Madison, James. "Federalist Papers: Primary Documents in American History." Research Guides at Library of Congress. Last modified 19, 2022. https://guides.loc.gov/federalist-papers/text-11-20.

71. Washington, George. "George Washington Letter 1790: Washington's Letter to the Jews of Newport." Touro Synagogue. Last

modified December 29, 2021. https://tourosynagogue.org/history/george-washington-letter/.

72. USA FACTS. "How Are Votes Counted?" USAFacts. Last modified September 14, 2022. https://usafacts.org/articles/how-are-votes-counted/.

73. ANES. American National Election Studies. Last modified April 13, 2023. https://electionstudies.org.

74. Ellis, Edward S. The Life of Colonel David Crockett: Comprising His Adventures as Backwoodsman and Hunter. Philadelphia, PA: Porter & Coates, 1984.

75. Library of Congress. "A Century of Lawmaking for a New Nation: U.S. Congressional Documents and Debates 1774-1875." Register of Debates, House of Representatives, 20th Congress, 1st Session. n.d. https://memory.loc.gov/ammem/amlaw/lwrdlink.html#anchor26. 2085-86.

76. Adams, Samuel. "Samuel Adams Heritage Society." Samuel Adams Heritage Society. Accessed May 8, 2023. https://www.samuel-adams-heritage.com/index.html.

77. Washington, George. "Farewell Address (1796)." National Constitution Center – Constitutioncenter.org. n.d. https://constitutioncenter.org/the-constitution/historic-document-library/detail/george-washington-farewell-address-1796.